BLINDSIDED

Recognizing and Dealing with
Passive-Aggressive Leadership
In the Workplace

PAULA M. DE ANGELIS, PhD

Contents

Disclaimer

The purpose of this book is to provide information about the negative effects of passive-aggressive leadership in the workplace on employees. Passive-aggressive behavior in company leaders appears to be a more prevalent problem than people might like to believe. It is hoped that this book will shed some light on the problem and give readers some ideas to think about, especially if they find themselves in work situations that are confusing, frustrating, dishonest, and full of mixed signals, or if they find that their career advancement is being blocked at all turns despite their hard work and productivity.It is not a psychological textbook nor is it a definitive source of information about passive-aggressive behavior in the workplace. Readers are encouraged to visit the websites listed at the end of the book for complementary and additional general information about passive-aggressive behavior.

Acknowledgments

This book would not have been possible without the support of my husband, family, friends, and colleagues from several different workplaces who shared their stories of passive-aggressive bosses and dysfunctional work environments. I also want to acknowledge the good leaders whom I have had the privilege of working for over the course of the last thirty years, because they showed me what assertive, constructive leadership is, which made it possible for me to recognize passive-aggressive, negative leadership.

In memory of my parents

Introduction

At this writing, I have been a full-time employee in the workforce for nearly thirty years, and have seen and experienced a lot in terms of how bosses and employees treat each other and what kinds of bosses are out there. Many of the experiences have been positive, uplifting, encouraging, and rewarding. Some of them have not. Some of the situations that have occurred between co-workers and between bosses and employees during these years have been strange, weird, and difficult to understand. Some of the situations had a considerable effect on me and my co-workers, on how we did our jobs, and on how we psychologically approached our jobs. I have worked as a research scientist in both academic and private research institutes during the past thirty years, both in the USA and in Norway. I have witnessed aggressive bosses behave rudely and coarsely towards their employees; I have witnessed passive bosses without a backbone or an interesting idea try to motivate employees who were bored beyond belief. This book is not about these types of bosses. It is primarily about passive-aggressive bosses and the negative effects of their behavior on their employees.

Although the literature seems to focus predominantly on how passive-aggressive employees make the workplace difficult for company management, the reverse is also true, that passive-aggressive management makes life in the workplace almost unbearable for the employees who must deal with that leadership on a daily basis. Employees who are the recipients of passive-aggressive behavior in the workplace often end up demoralized and in need of explanations that are not likely to be granted them. It is not always possible for them to sit down and figure out the dynamics of their work environment, especially a dysfunctional work environment. I have spent a fair amount of time trying to figure out my role in and my responses to some of the strange behavior in one of the workplaces in which I tried to function effectively, but what I have learned is that some of my own behavior was a response to passive-aggressive leadership in that workplace, and some of my responses, unfortunately, did not always work in my favor either professionally or psychologically. This book was begun as an attempt to make sense of that situation, and grew into an opportunity for me to analyze the different work environments I have experienced through the years. I decided to 'step back' from the suboptimal work environment and to watch what happened around me. I observed what went on for a one-year period in an objective and non-emotional way (as much as this was possible to do), and tried to figure out the dynamics of what was happening. It was exceedingly difficult to do, but I managed and learned a lot in the process, enough so that I decided to write this book in order to help those who face similar situations. My research background and experience helped make the task a bit easier, in that I am detail-oriented and have paid good attention to the intricacies of situations that have occurred to me and to others around me, even though I did not understand them immediately at the time they happened or despite my initial emotional response. I was also helped immeasurably by employees in different workplaces who shared their own stories of passive-aggressive leadership with me. I have not done an exhaustive study of different workplaces, nor have I thoroughly presented, discussed and assessed what is or is not a normal functioning work environment. I cannot provide detailed diagnoses or analyses of passive-aggressive individuals since I am neither a psychiatrist nor a psychologist. However, I can present some general characteristics of passive-aggressive behavior in company leaders and provide some objective observations of dysfunctional and frustrating passive-aggressive work environments.

I was initially interested in finding out what the experts had to say about passive-aggressive behavior in the workplace. There are a number of books available that deal with passive-aggressive behavior in a general context. Some of these books were geared towards passive-aggressive individuals in an attempt to get them to recognize specific character traits and behavior in themselves, which I gathered was a fairly difficult task. I was more interested in investigating how a passive-aggressive work environment affects its employees, or more precisely, the effect of passive-aggressive leadership on employees. I was quite surprised to find that there is actually a scarcity of books on exactly this subject. A Google search turned up a number of interesting hits and links to sites that contained original research articles written by psychologists, popular journalism, blogs and short reports that dealt with different aspects of workplace behavior, passive-aggressive behavior being one of them. However, the main focus of most of these articles was on passive-aggressive employees and less on passive-aggressive bosses. I hope to correct that in this book, since it has been my experience (and the experiences of others whose stories are presented in this book) that passive-aggressive leadership is a common scenario, much more common than perhaps company leadership wants to admit. It would actually make perfect sense that those who get promoted to leadership positions might often be those who on the surface appear to be agreeable, diplomatic, and nice, yet who are actually dishonest, backstabbing saboteurs behind the scenes. They will continue to behave in this way to keep the power they have achieved. I would like to see the results of a well-designed research study done on workplace environments, workplace behavior, and workplace dynamics. It is entirely possible that upper management can also be fooled by exactly the people they wish to promote, just as the employees of passive-aggressive bosses or co-workers of passive-aggressive individuals may have been fooled for years into doing their work for them, picking up the slack, compensating for their weaknesses and making them look good, all the while suffering in silence because to confront the passive-aggressive individual with any sort of frustration resulted in nothing, no recognition or acknowledgment of the problem, and hence no resolution. It also makes perfect sense to me that if passive-aggressive behavior in employees is a problem, it comes from somewhere. It may be that some employees are truly passive-aggressive and would be so in any work environment. But it may also be that passive-aggressive behavior on the part of employees is a reaction to a passive-aggressive boss. If an employee develops a passive-aggressive coping mechanism, a defense mechanism in response to a dysfunctional work environment, it may be the boss who is the problem, especially if the employee was not passive-aggressive from the start.

It takes time to learn to recognize passive-aggressive behavior for what it is, since passive-aggressive individuals are very good at making excuses and using lies to get out of potentially conflict-filled situations. This tells you how difficult passive-aggression can be to deal with in the workplace. The goal of this book is to raise the awareness of employees who work for passive-aggressive men and women. I'll attempt to characterize passive-aggressive behavior in leaders and to describe the views of work and the workplace held by those who suffer at the hands of passive-aggressive bosses. I will present stories from 'the front'--employees (who will remain anonymous) who have experienced passive-aggressive bosses over many years, describe the problems associated with working for (and with) passive-aggressive individuals and suggest some strategies for how to deal with them and with a passive-aggressive work environment in general.

I
Recognizing passive-aggressive behavior in workplace leaders

What do we know about passive-aggression? Up until the publication in 1994 of the fourth edition of The Diagnostic and Statistical Manual of Mental Disorders (DSM), a manual for mental health professionals published by the American Psychiatric Association, passive-aggression was classified as an Axis I (clinical) disorder with an organic (biological) basis (essentially nature as opposed to nurture). Examples of Axis I disorders are schizophrenia, bipolar disorder, panic, and anxiety. In the DSM-IV (1) passive-aggression was reclassified as an Axis II (non-organic) disorder, which means that the disorder is now considered to be the result of environmental influences rather than a biological disorder (essentially nurture as opposed to nature). The disorder does however have a biological component that can be treated clinically. The passive-aggressive personality disorder is described as a negativistic personality disorder, characterized by distinctive and pervasive patterns of negative attitudes and behavior, e.g. ambiguity, dishonesty, lying, resentment, and blaming others. Passive aggression is learned behavior in response to one's environment, and is often quite entrenched in an individual's personality. It is primarily a coping or defense mechanism in response to a dysfunctional environment. For the purposes of this book, I will focus on the behavioral aspects of passive aggression rather than on passive aggression as a personality disorder.

Passive-aggressive behavior in a boss or co-worker can cause considerable distress for employees who have to deal with these individuals on a daily basis. It becomes a major source of stress for an employee who may not understand how to tackle it. The main goal of this book is to present passive-aggressive behavior for what it is, dishonest and harmful behavior, such that employees working for a passive-aggressive boss (or together with a passive-aggressive co-worker) will be able to recognize this behavior for what it is in order to try to deal with it. I also want to attempt to explain some of the reasons for why passive-aggressive bosses behave the way they do towards their employees.

Extreme personality types are usually quite noticeable, and as a result, others can see what types of people they really are. There may also be consequences for extreme behavior, for example, that an overly-aggressive boss can be fired, or that a passive employee can also be fired if he or she is non-productive. Passive-aggressive individuals are difficult to control, difficult to 'read', and difficult to pin down. They survive and flourish in certain work environments, often with disastrous results for those who work for them. It is my contention that the passive-aggressive person who sits in a leadership position is actually worse for an employee's long-term self esteem than either an aggressive boss (excluding one who gets physical), or a passive boss. With these types of bosses, it is clear to you and your co-workers what types of people they are and what types of leadership styles they have. Passive-aggressive bosses are the most difficult to deal with because they can be well-liked by their peers and often seem to be quite effective and successful. Why this is the case is another story and one that I will deal with later in this book. It has to do with their ability to exploit the weaknesses and fears of those who work for them to their advantage. Try going out publicly against the passive-aggressive boss. Many people will say to you, "he or she is such a nice person, I can't believe he's really that way" or "I can't believe it's as bad as you describe" or "most of your problems are inside yourself" or "she's never been that way to me". If you hear this often enough over time, your self confidence will suffer. I guarantee it.

How do you feel at the hands of a passive-aggressive boss or co-worker? The word "**blindsided**" comes to mind. The definition of blindside is "to hit unexpectedly from or as if from the blind side; to surprise unpleasantly" (http://www.merriam-webster.com/dictionary/ blindsided). Thus blindsided describes how one might feel when dealing with a passive-aggressive boss. How many times have you come away from meetings or interactions with a boss or another co-worker, feeling as though you have been hit by a car that came out of nowhere? You just didn't see it coming. How many times have you been the butt of a joke that isn't funny or the recipient of undeserved comments, sarcasm and put-downs, and how many times have you wondered about the reason for this behavior? How many times have you ended up feeling used, duped, stabbed in the back, or the victim of dishonest behavior? How many times have you heard that same boss or co-worker describe himself or herself as a nice person (translated--one who tries to help others all the time, never says no to any request, tries to avoid conflict at all costs, one who wants to be liked by all, is not aggressive, never gets angry, is not tyrannical, is not verbally or physically abusive)?

A summary of some of the attitudes and behaviors that characterize passive-aggressive bosses (or co-workers) is presented in the next section. Using the traits and behaviors summarized here, I hope it will become somewhat easier to identify what some might call fairly typical behavior in the workplace as passive-aggressive behavior.

Attitudes/personality traits and corresponding behaviors/patterns of behavior in passive-aggressive leaders

1. Dishonest communicators

"COME TALK TO ME— LEAVE PATRICK ALONE."

Communication with employees is not direct or honest but rather indirect, dishonest, and ambiguous. Employees never get a clear sense of what was discussed, what conclusion was reached, what is expected of them, or what future strategy or plan was outlined. These types of bosses can talk non-stop but little of what they communicate is useful for employees or even remembered by the leaders themselves at future meetings. These leaders are poor listeners and poor communicators. They behave in an indecisive and impulsive manner, are forgetful, lack focus, and are unable to think long-term or systematically. They lack the skills needed to create an organized and rational plan of action for their employees.

2. Flip-floppers

SEE MATERIALITY COMMENTS SEE WORKPAPER FOR 1430

These types of leaders say one thing and then do the other. They change their minds frequently and cannot take a decisive stand on an issue. They forget what was decided upon, which confuses and frustrates those who prefer working with rational thinkers and leaders with the ability to strategize and make long-term plans.

3. Conflict-avoiders

ALL THE SOUTHERNERS

Passive-aggressive leaders dislike conflicts, arguments, disagreements, overt shows of anger, or confrontations. They become uncomfortable or embarrassed by shows of emotion, especially anger. It is possible to recognize anger in them as their faces will redden when confronted and when they are told things they do not like to hear, but otherwise they rarely exhibit overt anger. They view themselves as diplomatic individuals, and many of them have an obsessive need to be well-liked or seen as nice people. They dislike being confronted or having their opinions challenged, but seldom respond with overt anger. Instead they will 'punish' employees who initiate discussions or debates (seen as conflicts or arguments).

" JUST BREATHE"

4. Poor problem solvers

"WE'RE NOT ALL LIKE THAT!"

Passive-aggressive leaders avoid conflict as best they can. They are unable to resolve conflicts. They cannot or will not acknowledge the existence of workplace problems. They are good at using diversionary tactics to 'disarm' an employee who wants to discuss a serious problem, or they are good at 'diluting' an employee's concern about a specific issue. They do not really understand the value of problem resolution, negotiation, or compromise. *PAM*

5. Back-stabbers

"EYE-ROLLING" —

Passive-aggressive leaders are often envious of others who possess qualities they know they don't have or who achieve high levels of success. Their way of dealing with this is to joke about the inadequacies of others, especially if they have not achieved success in an area that the boss has, and they do this by making offhand, sarcastic, and spiteful comments. In this way, they never truly acknowledge or compliment another for the success that the other person has achieved. They cannot be honestly happy or enthusiastic about the successes of others. They can be back-stabbers behind the scenes and can try to sabotage others' attempts to get ahead. They have negative ideas concerning the talents/accomplishments of others, and do not like competition from others and especially from their employees. They are small-minded.

6. Control freaks   NO REFERENCE REQUIRED

Passive-aggressive leaders enjoy having control, power and prestige but will never admit to wanting or liking these. They have control issues, i.e. they want control but don't want to appear as though they are obsessed with having control. They will often try to convince others that these are not important to them and will often play down their career ambitions and need for control. They do however exhibit sullenness or resentment when or if power is taken from them, and will 'punish' attempts by employees to diminish their personal control and power. They have a strong need to be right about everything and expect compliance from employees.

7. Low levels of emotional intelligence   NO LEADERSHIP QUALITIES

Passive-aggressive leaders have self esteem and confidence issues. They act as though they have high levels of self confidence but in reality they don't. They can dominate a work environment with a false bravado, creating the false and confusing impression that they have high levels of self confidence. They are good poseurs, good actors. They are disingenuous, and many are more extroverted than introverted. They often have a low emotional quotient (EQ). They often lack tact and self insight. They have poorly-functioning social antenna when it comes to daily dealings with employees, and can be disrespectful but often in a jovial way. They joke excessively (usually at the expense of other people's feelings/reputations), and cannot genuinely apologize for their bad behavior because they lack the insight necessary to understand that they have crossed the line over to inappropriate behavior.

Most passive-aggressive leaders will exhibit many of the traits and behaviors listed here, according to my observations and personal experiences and the experiences of others who have shared their stories with me. A boss who exhibits a certain bravado will often act quite friendly and outgoing and create an initial impression on a new employee that he or she is open and available to that employee for support, despite the fact that this person is actually a poor listener, a poor problem-solver, and socially superficial. Overall, a superficial and nonchalant approach to nearly all real problems defines the passive-aggressive boss. His or her indifference spells problems for the employees who have to deal with this type of boss. Honest attempts at real communication are essentially wasted on this person. He or she will not remember the gist of important conversations, will forget what was ultimately decided, and will have to be reminded of what he or she actually did promise in terms of helping an employee. They often view employees as existing solely to help them and do not see them as real individuals with opinions and minds of their own. These bosses enjoy the power their behavior has over their employees and are not genuinely interested in helping an employee advance further. This may not be surprising since if an employee advances, the end result will be that this boss loses his or her 'meal-ticket'. It is my opinion that passive-aggressive behavior on the part of a boss towards an employee actually sabotages an employee's chance of advancing in this work environment. It is difficult to get these types of bosses to understand that they actually have the power to help their employees. They are so preoccupied with their own work situations that they are unable to empathize or put themselves in an employee's place to really try to understand how their employees experience things. I do not believe that a passive-aggressive boss is always aware of how detrimental his or her behavior is to the respective employees who have to deal with it on a daily basis, but I cannot believe that they behave in this way without an underlying motive, which may or may not be clear to them. The question is just how conscious or aware of his or her behavior a passive-aggressive boss actually is. Does this person understand what he or she is doing most of the time (or some of the time) and why? Does this person have 'glimpses' of self-insight, and if yes, do they scare or jolt him or her? It is difficult to get answers to these questions since passive-aggressive bosses will never admit to their passive-aggressive behavior. Herein lies the problem, since without acknowledgment of the behavior on the part of the person practicing it, it is nearly impossible to change the behavior.

Passive-aggressive leaders are intelligent enough to have learned enough about their workplace environment (without having dissected or studied it in detail) to know exactly where they fit and/or how they want to fit into it. Passive-aggressive behavior in the workplace is practiced by reasonably intelligent people who have 'learned' that passive behavior in the workplace spells death for their advancement and that aggressive behavior in the workplace is not welcomed or rewarded for the most part. The only employees who truly get away with purely aggressive behavior are those who sit at the top and run the entire show, those who can hire and fire at will. Passive-aggressive individuals often behave in a morally relative way, i.e. they are not particularly attached to any personal philosophy or code of ethics and cannot (or will not) take a real stand on a serious issue. They dislike, resent (and can punish in indirect ways) employees who try to 'force' them to take a stand on a particular issue or to solve a particular problem. It is this aspect of their behavior that makes them quite difficult and frustrating to deal with. You never quite know where you have them and you cannot really rely on them when you need them. The only thing consistent about them is their passive-aggressive behavior pattern, which is characterized by indirect aggression (2), dishonesty, need for control, need to be well-liked, and dislike of conflict, all of which are bound to create difficulties in the workplace in the long run. Despite their deficient emotional intelligence, passive-aggressive individuals manage to pay enough attention to others such that they learn to 'read' other people's weaknesses and to act upon that knowledge accordingly so that it benefits them. They can behave in this way without being particularly conscious of their own sneaky behavior, or without giving that impression at least, which makes it very difficult to deal with them or to try to get them to change their behavior patterns. Simply put, they react to their work environment in a way that feels viscerally correct without always truly understanding the subtleties or choices involved. They adopt complex behavior patterns and reactions without always understanding them, but are intelligent enough to understand that they work. How do they understand this? Because they are rewarded for their leadership behavior 'style' in the standard ways one might be rewarded at work--promotions, salary increases, prestige, praise, recognition, and titles. This is what I mean when I say that passive-aggressive leaders are not stupid. They know how to defend their turf and protect themselves against the comments or requirements of others.

Passive-aggressive leaders maintain that they communicate well, but in fact they do not manage real and honest communication very well. I describe many passive-aggressive leaders as Teflon bosses, because nothing sticks. They don't remember important conversations or pertinent information. They don't remember important decisions, outcomes of meetings, or even that a meeting occurred. They are chronically late for meetings or forget that they scheduled them. They don't write down notes from meetings, and they can be sardonic about others who do. They are good at delegating work to others only to forget that they did so. They are very good at projecting their weaknesses onto others, and they may do it in a way that appears humorous to others who don't know them or have dealings with them. Dealing with passive-aggressive bosses or co-workers is an exercise in frustration. A typical scenario would be that a passive-aggressive boss forgot an important conversation or meeting and would explain it away by saying how busy he is such that he forgot the time, or that those working for him forgot to remind him about the meeting. Discussions concerning project planning, strategy, organization and problem resolution are often fruitless and eventually pointless because he or she forgets what was discussed a week or two ago, so that each new conversation is really just a re-hash of previous conversations and presentations. Attempts at honest or direct conversations with them may backfire because they will remember exactly what they want to remember, namely that you dared to criticize or confront them, but they will not remember, nor will they do anything about, the actual problem you came into their office to discuss with them. Problems do not get solved because 'there are no real problems'. It is thus a given that there are plenty of problems in a passive-aggressive workplace. In fact, the initial reaction of a passive-aggressive boss to an employee's attempt to bring a problem to light is to be passive and to dismiss the importance of any problem that is brought up, but still the boss may thank his employee for bringing up the problem and even seem eager to discuss ways to solve that problem while the employee is sitting in his office. The aggressive reaction comes later, and it comes in a dishonest way. Once the employee leaves the room, the problem leaves with him. The boss no longer has to think about it or be concerned about it, and may even resent the employee afterwards for discussing the problem with him or her. Woe to the employee who confronts the passive-aggressive boss in an assertive, honest way about the boss's behavior or failures. That employee will be the recipient of a lot of 'crazy-making' behavior in the future. That is guaranteed. The passive-aggressive boss for the most part cannot see his or her own problems, as he or she lacks the insight to do so, and/or lacks the motivation and discipline necessary to undertake the task of learning to know oneself. If confronted with the frustrations of co-workers concerning their behavior, these bosses immediately feel hurt because really, he or she is such a nice person (translated--why is everyone picking on me, why are people angry at me? now you're being unfair to me). They don't understand why people get angry at them and until confronted or told directly, really don't see or feel the anger from others. They do not take kindly to the fact that a co-worker or employee would confront them on their behavior. Passive-aggressive bosses will often say how little it means to them to have power, but that statement is also dishonest. Most of them enjoy having power and have unique (and often destructive) ways of holding onto that power. How they got this way may have something to do with the work environment they themselves 'grew up' in, i.e. they may at one point have been unable to cope with their workplace situation, and learned to use passive-aggressive behavior as a coping mechanism to deal with their work environment.

Persistent patterns of passive-aggressive behavior

A boss who consistently behaves in a passive-aggressive manner towards his employees will create a work environment that will be defined by some of the following behaviors and situations. Some readers may say that this is fairly common behavior and that I am simply describing 'normal' workplace behavior. I emphasize that it is the **'regular and persistent pattern of behavior'** that counts, and it is that pattern of behavior that I am talking about here. It is only over time that attentive employees begin to understand the dynamics of their work environment. It is only over time that these same employees begin to see the correlation between their inner turmoil and confusion and their work environment. These employees have possibly dealt with a passive-aggressive boss for years and perhaps are only starting to understand the reasons for why they feel so demoralized and exhausted. Others may feel bitter or frustrated. The common theme, if employees talk among themselves, and many of them do, but often only after several years of isolated suffering, is that nearly all of them share the same feelings about their boss. The boss has regularly let them all down over time. I have seen this happen in two completely different work environments. Over time, employees 'woke up' to what was going on. Some quit, some stayed put and learned to put their guard up whenever they had to deal with their boss, and some decided just not to care too much anymore about their jobs.

Some of these persistent passive-aggressive behavior patterns on the part of bosses towards employees include the following:

1. Disrespectful of the plans and schedules of others

— WALKS IN LOUDLY — NO REGARD FOR ISSUE AT HAND —

Passive-aggressive leaders can plan meetings with employees/co-workers and consistently show up late for them without informing employees that they would be late. They always have some excuse (often the same excuse) for being late, that employees simply must accept. It could be that they 'forgot' the meeting. They expect employees to always be available to them on a moment's notice. This happens on a regular basis.

"LET ME DRIVE!" (TOOK OVER MY MOUSE!)

2. Constantly say yes (cannot say no)

Passive-aggressive leaders constantly say yes to new projects and the additional work that is entailed. They cannot say no to others who want help or work done (passive reaction) despite the fact that they are quite aware of (and may even be irritated by) the fact that they are overwhelming themselves and their respective employees with more work than can rationally be handled. They cannot be honest enough to say "No, we cannot manage that right now". The 'aggressive' reaction can be taken out on employees who must handle the extra workload (and who may have tried to get the boss to see that the requests were unreasonable), and not on those who made the unreasonable requests. This happens on a regular basis.

3. Unable to prioritize work projects

Passive-aggressive leaders bite off more than they can chew and expect employees to do the same. They resent employees who do not want to do this and 'punish' them accordingly. Nothing is a greater source of frustration for an employee than hearing about yet another new and exciting project that the boss wants to prioritize at the expense of the other projects that were also top-priority perhaps a week ago. These bosses also forget what has been decided upon in previous meetings, and take up the same topics for discussion as were discussed previously. After a new round of discussions, the outcome can be quite different than what was originally decided. Everything is fluid, nothing is definite. They are poor decision-makers. All doors must be left open in case some opportunity pops up that supersedes all others. These types of bosses have a 'grass is always greener on the other side' mentality when it comes to work projects. If it's trendy or hot, they'll consider it. An employee's honest dedication and long hours spent planning and organizing projects or working on problem resolution are pointless because a passive-aggressive boss can change his or her mind on a whim, end projects immediately, start new projects without any plan or design, or forget what was discussed a week ago, so that each new meeting is really just a re-hash of what occurred before. This happens on a regular basis.

4. They are always so busy

Passive-aggressive leaders always make a point out of how busy they are (translated--they are very important). The implication is that others are not as busy as they are or that others, since they are 'less busy' (no one could possibly be as busy as they are), can just shove current projects aside without problems. No one is as important as the boss. They expect employees to pick up the slack and to work extra hours without extra pay (they will never suggest extra pay for extra work). They must look good regardless of whether their employees are appropriately compensated for their extra work. The irony of this is that the employees who work for this boss often stay overtime and work long hours anyway as a matter of principle, since they usually have a strong work ethic.

5. Take sole credit for ideas and project outcome

Passive-aggressive leaders rely on others to help them make important decisions but take full credit for the eventual outcome. They exploit the loyalty and hard work of others to look good without giving credit where credit is due. They are power-hungry but not obvious about it, i.e., they are very good at verbalizing that having power does not matter to them, but not good at putting into practice what they say. They will not delegate power to others or give away the power they have, but they are very adept at 'delegating' (as they define it) the menial (scut) work and responsibility for the outcome of an important project to their employees in order to evade doing the low-level work themselves. They then take full credit for the project outcome. In other words, they delegate all the real work away to others and take full credit for the results. In a one-on-one situation with an employee, they are unable to compliment the employee in any real fashion without being offhand, indifferent, or sarcastic (in a joking way).

6. Use of sarcasm and joking

[handwritten: DAILY "OUR GREAT LEADER"]

Passive-aggressive leaders use sarcasm to 'attack' an employee but react with surprise when called on it. They didn't 'mean it' that way and the employee comes out looking like the bad guy for trying to defend himself. They will let an employee know in an offhand or sarcastic way if the employee is too ambitious, too idealistic or reaches too high (the employee should know his or her place). The employee should never think that he is worth something in his own right without the boss, or that he is better than the boss in any way. They can compliment an employee in front of others if that means that the others will see the boss in a good light--as a nice and generous person. This preserves the image of themselves as nice people.

7. Don't rock the boat

[handwritten: YES! RESISTANT TO CHANGE! IMPROVEMENT]

Passive-aggressive leaders are invested in preserving the status quo as long as it benefits them and their position in the workplace. Employees who rock their boat or the status quo are seen as troublemakers and need to be 'tamed' or 'forced' to toe the line.

8. Play the 'divide and conquer' game to retain their control

[handwritten: PLAYS NICE W/ 'CRUELA']

Passive-aggressive leaders play the 'divide and conquer' game with employees by talking about each of them behind their backs but never directly to them. In this way, the boss releases the anger he or she maintains he or she doesn't feel, just not directly to the person he or she is angry at. This type of behavior I've witnessed mostly in female bosses, but some male bosses are very good at it as well.

All of this behavior is negative behavior, since it is neither constructive nor encouraging. The unrelenting nature of this behavior destroys employee morale, confidence, the desire to do a good job, and ultimately productivity. It creates confusion, frustration, resentment, anxiety, and fear in employees who are recipients of this behavior. Thus it is not surprising that passive-aggressive behavior is defined as negativistic.

II
Real-life examples of passive-aggressive bosses and workplaces

You may find yourself in work situations that make you feel uncomfortable for a variety of reasons. You feel that you are being ignored and passed over for promotions and projects in favor of others whom you are told are more suitable. You know that things are going on behind your back but that you are being kept in the dark about them. You feel that there is an undercurrent of dishonesty and political game-playing going on. These games may not directly concern you but you know that they have a negative impact on the work environment. You ask your boss about specific incidents, problems or comments and are told that you have misinterpreted them. If they concern you specifically and you ask about them, you are told that you are paranoid or negative. You feel frustrated, irritated, and a little off-center.

The following short stories are representative examples of passive-aggressive behavior in the workplace and are based on actual situations that have occurred in several different workplaces over the course of my thirty years in the workforce. I have been witness to some of them; others stories have been told to me. What most of them have in common is that each employee who was the recipient of his or her boss' passive-aggressive behavior initially reacted with surprise, disbelief, and disappointment. They were blindsided. In certain cases, the situations repeated themselves and the employees involved began to feel abused, frustrated and angry. In most cases, even when employees asserted themselves and demanded respect, the pattern of behavior on the part of the passive-aggressive boss did not change. Most of the affected employees figured out, after a long while on the job, that each day meant a new confusing situation, a new fight for respect, and the likelihood that they would not get respect that day or perhaps ever.

Some real-life stories of passive-aggressive behavior in bosses and workplaces

1. Sabotaging employee advancement--taking full credit and retaining control   *DOES NOT GIVE 'ATTA BOYS'*

A boss informs an employee that they will 'share' leadership on an upcoming project. They will be co-leaders. The employee takes the bait, organizes the entire project and does most of the actual work involved, at the request of the boss who claims he is too busy (translated "too important") to get involved in the nuts and bolts of the project. The project is completed, and the boss ends up with sole credit for the outcome. The employee receives no substantial recognition for his co-leadership on the project from company management and wonders why. He later comes to discover that company management was never informed by his boss that the project had two leaders. This is dishonest behavior that sabotages the employee's chance of getting the recognition and rewards that he deserves. The boss retains the control and power that is so important to him and gets away with not having to do any of the tedious work involved or with having to share the rewards with his 'co-leader'.

2. Sabotaging employee advancement--taking full credit (version 2)

A boss schedules an important meeting with project collaborators but 'forgets' to inform the one employee on the team who has done the most amount of work on the project about it because he couldn't 'find' him. That employee doesn't find out about the meeting until it is over (and he also finds out that some members of upper management were present), and his boss comes with the excuse that he forgot to tell him, but that he will remember next time, and anyway, the meeting wasn't really that important so the employee really didn't need to be there. Of course, the meeting was important and the employee should have been there, because the boss will take credit for the work that the employee has done and for which the employee should be recognized.

3. Sabotaging employee advancement--keeping the employee down

A boss 'leaks' information to his employee that has implications for the employee's future chance at building up his own team, since it is time for the employee to advance in the organization. This involves being able to hire a person that the employee has 'headhunted' and recommended to company management. The boss informs the employee that company management is interested in hiring this person but that they need more background information for this person. He tells the employee to provide management with this information. The employee does this, even though he thinks it a bit strange that management didn't directly contact him to ask him personally to send this information. He sends the requested information to management, but hears nothing from them for several months. He finally gets a letter from management saying that the headhunted candidate lost out to another applicant for the job. His boss calls him into his office to confirm this. The employee wonders a bit as to the reason, since he was given the impression that this candidate had the job for all intents and purposes (according to his boss). He finds out from his boss that his actions (providing the 'requested' information) irritated management (again management didn't take direct contact with him) because they did not like that the employee 'found out' that this person had a good chance of being hired. It was never revealed that the employee was told to take contact with management and the employee doesn't really understand (at that point) what happened (he has been blindsided). The employee thinks it is hard enough to deal with the feelings of disappointment and frustration and it takes about a year for him to understand what really happened. When he looks back on the situation at a later time, he understands that he fell into his boss' trap. This was the boss' way of keeping him down and of punishing him for trying to build a team of his own. When he tells the story to other people outside his company, all of whom are managers themselves, he understands that his gut instincts were correct--that his boss was trying to hold him down and succeeded. He remains at the company, but management never really does find out who leaked the information to the employee. But the employee has learned his lesson and is more on his guard for the future.

4. Always late and always an excuse

A boss schedules a meeting with an employee, which will also include a colleague who is coming in from out of town. They agree to first meet at 1 pm, but at 1 pm the colleague has not arrived and they re-schedule for 2 pm. The colleague arrives at 2 pm and the boss calls up to the employee (who has pushed aside a lot of other work that day to accommodate the meeting) and says they won't be up until 3 pm. The employee says that will be fine. Quitting time is at 5 pm. She has often worked overtime but today she has made other plans so she has to leave at 5 pm. At 4 pm she calls down to say that she is waiting for them and could they please come up to start the meeting because she has to leave at 5 pm. They finally show up at 4:45 pm and come into the employee's office expecting to have an hour's length meeting. This type of situation, where the boss showed up late for meetings with no valid excuse whatsoever, had happened countless times before. At those times she had felt mistreated but never did anything about it. Her boss was always offhand about most things and didn't understand why his employees became irritated with him for this type of behavior. It was just who he was. She and other employees were just expected to sit there and to accept his disrespectful, passive-aggressive behavior. After many such episodes, this employee decides to stand up for herself. At 5 pm, the employee gets up, puts on her jacket and says that she has to leave, which she must do because of her prearranged plans for Friday evening. Her boss gets red in the face (indication of anger but does not show it) at this announcement. Both the boss and his colleague continue to sit there until she picks up her briefcase and wishes them a good weekend. By then they get the message that she really is leaving. Up until that point, the boss was sure she would just stick around for as long as it would take for them to be finished. What is really going on here, and why is this passive-aggressive behavior on the part of the boss? The boss is really saying that his time is more valuable than his employee's time, and that she should just wait around until he decides the time to have a meeting. In other words, he wants complete control and resents the fact that she called down to ask where they were. He didn't like the fact that she had called down and been assertive in her request that they come up to start the meeting. He felt that she was controlling the situation (and trying to control him) and punished her by showing up late for the meeting. His way of viewing it would be that he showed up when HE wanted to show up and that she was simply required to accept that. He will also 'punish' her eventually for getting up and leaving the meeting at 5 pm.

5. Gaining control of the team

A boss is worried that she is losing control over one (strong-willed) person on her team and attempts to destroy the reputation of that employee by 'gossiping' to another employee about that person. How she does this is through barbed comments, sarcasm, or feigned concern to another co-worker on the team, e.g. "So and so is looking pretty drained today and her work is not up to par. I'm sorry you have to pick up the slack—I guess her marriage problems are taking their toll on her and affecting her work. That's too bad". How is the co-worker who is privy to this information and purported concern supposed to respond to this statement? For the first, perhaps this co-worker knew nothing (and didn't want to know either) about the other co-worker's personal life. For the second, the boss gains power over this person because she is establishing a confidence with that person, sharing a secret. For the third, this co-worker feels guilty for being privy to confidential information, which may or may not be true, but the boss has damaged that person's reputation simply by suggesting that such and such may be the case. This is dishonest behavior and game playing with often destructive outcomes. There is no respect shown to the individual employees involved and no loyalty either. This is insidious game playing because it can take some time for the employees to figure out what is going on and to understand the game that is being played. And understanding the game playing does not necessarily lead to a cessation of the game playing. This is passive-aggressive behavior on the part of the boss because the boss doesn't confront the employee directly with what appears to be a problem, namely that the boss feels that the employee is a little too strong-willed. She goes behind the employee's back and tries to destroy her that way.

6. Making an employee feel worthless

An employee asks for a (well-deserved) raise and is told that there is no extra money in the budget that year to cover it. Her boss (a man) says that he wishes he could do something about the situation, but he cannot because he has no real power or influence with company management when it comes to these types of decisions. He really doesn't like this employee very much because she speaks her mind. The employee knows that this is not true, because the boss has just worked extremely hard to arrange extra payment for a more favored employee (a man) in the same group. Both employees are married with children. Word gets back to the female employee that the male employee got his raise because he had a family to support, and this is later confirmed by the boss at a group meeting where the favored employee is praised to the hilt. When she brings up the fact that she also has a family to support, her assertiveness is dismissed in the typically offhand way that her boss has with her when he thinks she is being selfish and not a team player. He'll say something akin to "don't be envious" or "the world is an unfair place". Her assertiveness and the fact that she dared to comment on the situation has been misinterpreted as envy, which it clearly is not. His actions and words tell her—"I like this male employee better; he is nicer to me (translated, more compliant and therefore worth more to me) than you are, so I will support his request for extra money". It is all done without any arguments whatsoever.

7. Making an employee feel worthless (version 2)

A boss comes into his employee's office to report that a new job position is available in his group. The position will be announced shortly and the boss casually shows the employee, who is a senior member of the team, the annual salary that he is considering offering the new employee who would join the team in an apprentice position. The annual salary is substantially more than the senior employee is making. The senior employee comments on the irregularity of offering a newcomer so much money, and mentions that he has not yet achieved that salary level, so he feels that it would be unfair to him and to other members of the group to offer a newcomer such a high salary. The boss' response is to tell him that he is envious and unwilling to make the team as good as it could be. The boss shows no understanding whatsoever (very low EQ) for the views of the senior employee and in fact is irritated that this employee asserted himself by criticizing the boss. The boss leaves the office, and the employee knows that it could very well happen that the new employee will make more than all of the other current team members. However, he and the team will never know for sure what the outcome actually was. He also has to wonder why the boss could be so callous in his treatment of a loyal hard-working employee. He concludes that the boss is either trying to hurt him, put him in his place (or try to keep him there), or that he lacks so much insight and empathy that he simply is unable to understand how his behavior will impact negatively on members of his team.

8. Exploiting a talented employee

A boss and an employee agree on the design and implementation of a new project and that the employee will act as project leader. A few months pass, the results start to come in, and the project seems slated for success. The employee has worked hard on generating results, testing new methodologies and strategies, and fully expects the boss' support when it comes time to discuss project results and outcome. He also could reasonably expect to receive the major credit associated with the project's success. The boss arranges a group meeting so that the employee can present his results to the group. During the discussion that follows his presentation, suggestions are raised by the boss as to how these results can be used to further the projects of some of the other group members. Instead of complimenting the employee who has achieved the good results, the boss takes the results and essentially redistributes them to other member(s) of the group who have not been involved in the project at all. The employee feels that he is losing control of his project, and sure enough, after a few months, he has lost ownership of the project. It has essentially been given to another employee in the group whose contribution to the project has been negligible, and often ineffective if there has been any contribution at all. This 'transfer' of project ownership takes place very slowly, indirectly and quietly. Any attempts to right this situation by the employee in question are met with comments about the employee's aggressiveness, competitiveness and inability to function as a team player. When this happens on two separate occasions, the employee knows he cannot trust the boss or even his co-workers, since none of the latter ever react negatively to the boss' suggestion that another person 'overtake' the project. The employee realizes that his boss is using him to generate results without any intention of giving him full credit for his work. He also realizes that his intelligence and drive are being exploited by his boss who understands that he can relax and let this employee carry most of the weight and responsibility for project success that would otherwise fall on his shoulders.

9. Always too busy for a meeting

An employee works for a boss who is quite busy and never seems to find enough time to discuss work projects with him. The boss is always on the run, with a smile on his face. The boss doesn't really like this employee however, because he thinks he is too direct and too much to handle. He leaves notes on the employee's desk with instructions as to what is to be done that day or that week. When the employee tries to get an audience with the boss, he is always dismissed with a smile and the same response--'the boss is busy but he'll get back to you as soon as possible'. This never happens. The employee does the best he can to follow the instructions presented but of course his work is subsequently criticized at group meetings because he hasn't had a chance to check out specific aspects of the work assignments with his boss.

10. Playing the 'your opinion counts' game

An employee is asked for his opinions and meanings, and works on drafting a report as he was asked to do, only to find out when he delivers the report (in a timely way) that the boss has already made his decision without his input after all. So why did he ask for the employee's input? This behavior is designed to inform the employee that his time and effort are worth very little to the boss, nor are his opinions. He should just be available at will. Asking the employee for input, however, makes the boss seem like a 'nice guy' and a good leader.

11. Playing the 'thanks for sharing' game

Alternatively, an employee volunteers his opinions about how to tackle and change a particular work situation. He is asked by his boss to put his thoughts on paper and to submit them to the boss. This he does. When he hands it to his boss, his boss thanks him and says that he did a good job. When the employee leaves his office, the boss reads his report and then promptly buries it, since it is either involves too much effort, is too critical of current management, or too direct. Or the boss may not read it at all. Either way, the report gets buried. The employee will never find out (even if he asks) why his report was ignored. The employee will in fact never get any feedback at all concerning his report, and he may eventually feel ignored by company management, but he won't understand why at first. As time goes on, he will understand that because he dared to think that he had a good idea and did something about it, he was 'punished' by being ignored. Or perhaps he is being ignored because he was perceived as critical of the company and of management. And by ignored, I mean, overlooked for project leadership, salary increases, or more challenging positions.

12. Playing the 'make the employee wait' game

EVERY TIME YOU GO IN

An employee has given his boss important documents to sign. They might be documents having to do with an employee taking vacation, going on sick leave, or transferring to another department. They require immediate action. Or perhaps an employee needs a decision from the boss concerning specific and pressing issues. The boss takes an inordinate amount of time to sign the papers or make the decision. Why would he do this? Again, this type of boss knowingly procrastinates because he can, and because he knows that if he sits on the papers for a while, maybe this particular issue will go away or diminish in importance, especially if it is an issue that irritates him with regard to this particular employee. As far as he's concerned, the documents can just join the other piles of paper on his desk. Why is he behaving in this way? He might be irritated at the employee for wanting to take vacation (or maternity leave, or sick leave) exactly now, but he cannot say that directly to the employee. He doesn't want an outright confrontation with her. He knows that she needs (or wants) the documents back from him immediately. He decides that it's good for her to learn patience and that she doesn't need to get her way immediately. He feels that the employee should be reminded of who is the boss, that the employee should remember her place. If the employee reminds him that he promised to get the papers signed and back to her, the boss can simply say he'll get around to it. He may even ask the employee in a joking way, "Don't you trust me"?

13. Withholding positive feedback and praise

An employee writes a good report that is generally well-received by his peers. One of his colleagues asks him for a copy of the report, and tells him that he also wants another copy for his own boss, who had expressed an interest in reading it after hearing his employee mention that it had just been published. The employee gives his colleague copies of the report. He hears nothing from his colleague's boss, not about receiving the report nor does he get any feedback about what his colleague's boss thought of the report. His colleague's boss happens to be a man whom the employee had previously sought employment with, and who had repeatedly promised the employee that he would eventually hire him but that it would take some time to arrange a job for him, which never happened. No job ever materialized. The employee understands that this is just one more example of the passive-aggressive nature of this particular boss. He lied to the employee originally about wanting to hire him and the issue just 'faded' away, and he now 'ignores' the same employee's achievements. In other words, he doesn't really care about this employee at all, unless there was a chance to exploit the employee for his own gain, which he has attempted to do on another occasion.

14. Ignoring/bypassing the right employee for the job

A top leader is considering two candidates for a position, both of whom have expressed an interest in filling it. One candidate is better-suited for the position because she is 'closer to the floor' and has extensive experience with daily operations, which is what the position requires. The other candidate is her immediate boss (a man), who is less qualified for the actual position but who has more administrative experience, which the position does not really require. The boss gets the job but makes sure that everyone around him knows that his employee is "as qualified" for the job as he is. This is small consolation for the employee who really felt that she deserved the position. Several years go by and the employee discovers that her boss and the company leader made a deal between them--her boss would get the job in exchange for providing a specific service for the company leader. This was all done behind the scenes and no one else knew about it. The leader eventually retires, and a new (and younger) leader comes onboard as his replacement. This new leader has been a part of the team of the former leader and knows him very well. He lets slip to the employee that it wasn't possible to rule out that the former leader had tried to hold her down by giving the position (that she deserved) to her boss. Again, this employee remained at the company, aware of what happened and on her guard for future such occurrences. She now knows that she cannot trust her boss to tell the truth. She also understands that her boss is actually competing with her, and that he wants the power and prestige of such a position despite saying that he doesn't.

15. Pulling the rug out from under the employee

An employee (mid-management level) has functioned as team leader for quite a while. Due to a massive company reorganization, all employees are told that there may be restructuring and that all levels of management should expect changes to leadership structure. This employee is told not to worry however by upper management--his position is safe. He finds himself however eventually replaced by a new leader that upper management simply informs him of one day by email. He is not prepared for this eventuality especially after management told him not to worry. He still is able to keep his job but he loses leadership of his team. He has little recourse but to carry on and accept the decision even though he doesn't like it. This scenario would be more common in a passive-aggressive workplace where all levels of upper management behave in passive-aggressive ways.

16. Don't expect the boss' support

An employee has worked hard on a scientific research project and prepares a slide presentation for upper management so that he can discuss his work. His boss has basically given the work his stamp of approval and had very few comments to the preliminary draft of the presentation that the employee showed him. The employee was hoping for some quality feedback but didn't get much. In fact, the boss has been so busy that the employee always felt that he was bothering the boss by asking him for his feedback and opinions. The day arrives for the employee's presentation, and he presents his work, but some upper managers respond to his presentation by unfairly and unnecessarily criticizing the work in a most unprofessional manner. The employee defends his results, but feels very unsure about the situation. He waits for his boss to step in and defend him and the work, but his boss remains silent. When the employee refers some of the questions and negative remarks to his boss, the boss responds by telling those present that he was not aware that the employee had done this or that, or gone down that particular avenue of investigation, and that he agrees with the criticism for the most part. The employee expects support from his boss but doesn't get it. After the meeting is over, the boss tells the employee that he should have discussed the presentation with the boss first before he presented the work. The lecture wasn't presented the way the boss wanted it to be presented. The employee is never told HOW he should have presented the work; it's just assumed that the correct way would have been the boss' way. The employee feels blown off and betrayed, and casts about for explanations for the boss' behavior. The only explanation he can come up with is that his boss is primarily interested in avoiding any sort of conflict, especially with upper management. He wants to preserve his reputation and the status quo and look good to company management. He is not too worried about the fact that he didn't defend his employee and his work. This is a crazy-making situation because the employee never really knows why the boss didn't stand up for him. He does know that he consulted the boss for advice before he gave the presentation. He knows that the work is good, because it is eventually published and international response indicates that the work is very good. Why didn't the boss stand up for his employee? Of course, the boss (and upper management as well) goes on to gain from this work, and all is apparently forgotten. But the employee does not forget how his boss behaved and that he felt completely unsupported. This type of behavior is characteristic of a boss who hates any sort of 'conflict' and will avoid them at all costs.

17. *"You scratch my back and I'll scratch yours" (and the employee loses)* Pam & Sharron

A boss has a colleague who calls him requesting help (information and data) on a project proposal that he is writing. The boss knows that this colleague is working on a similar type of project as one of his employees, who has invested a lot of time in this project. The boss and his colleague are cronies ("you scratch my back and I'll scratch yours") rather than competitors, and the boss agrees to give his colleague some of the data that has been generated by his employee to use in his project proposal. The idea is that these data will strengthen his proposal. The employee however is never asked either for his permission to use his data or for his opinion about using it, and hears from the boss the next day that this is what transpired. The employee becomes angry and tells the boss what he thinks of the situation, that he disliked being told after the fact, and was not considered in the equation. The entire situation reflects exactly what the boss and his colleague think of the employee, and how low down on the totem pole they consider him to be. Apart from expressing his displeasure about the situation to his boss, there is little else the employee can do, except confront the colleague in question (as well as his boss) and make clear that this type of behavior will not be tolerated in the future. In reality, the employee can only hope that this type of situation will not repeat itself.

18. Message to new employee--you're not better than anyone else

ASHLEY'S AREA OF EXPERTISE

A company headhunts and recruits a male employee based upon his well-known international reputation. The leaders promise him a leadership position, technical and financial support, and considerable office space. On his first day on the job, he arrives at his new workplace only to discover that nothing of what has been promised to him is in place or ready for him. The company leaders are traveling and are not present to greet him, he has no office to move into, and his 'team' of assistants is non-existent. He finds out very quickly that he is going to have to 'fight' for everything he's been promised or simply accept that this is the way business is done at his new company. This type of behavior borders on fraud--the new employee is recruited under false pretenses. The company needs him to bolster their international reputation. They will eventually get around to giving him what they promised, but on their terms and time schedule. He is simply going to have to wait or else quit. And since company management is united in their treatment of the new employee, there is no one he can really complain to in the hopes of righting the obvious wrongs done to him. The leaders will never acknowledge that they have treated him badly or dishonestly. They will find appropriate excuses for why things were not ready for him and why he was treated so unprofessionally. This is the crux of passive-aggressive behavior--such behavior is always right on the border of what is acceptable and not acceptable. A passive-aggressive person and/or organization can never really be taken for their 'bad' behavior; rather, they always seem to 'get away' with it.

19. Stalling tactics ('promises, promises')

A company decides to focus on a particular project and appoints one of their local experts as project leader. They promise him help on the project in the form of two assistants that will be available to him full-time. The only problem is that these assistants are already working full-time on other projects. They are given permission to start working for the project leader on such and such a date and both of them work hard to finish up their current assignments so that they can start work for the new project leader. That day arrives, but they still have not managed to finish up their current work assignments, and in fact have been given several new assignments to work on. The project leader waits for six months for his 'help' to materialize, and then it dawns slowly on him that this is not going to happen. Either management decided that the project wasn't worth the time and monetary investment, or that the project leader could manage his project alone. But he is never given an explanation one way or the other. He simply must figure out on his own what he thinks is going on. There are no written contracts, no emails, no paper trails to show that there was in fact a deal between him and management that he was promised help. Eventually he understands that he will not be able to fulfill the project requirements alone and mentions that to his boss, who again promises that very soon, he will have the help he needs. This type of situation could have led to a passive-aggressive reaction on the employee's part, namely that the employee decides to stall the project until he gets the help he needs. It did not, however. This is the insidious nature of passive-aggressive management. In the long run, it can lead to passive aggressive reactions in employees, such that an entire workplace can become passive-aggressive over time.

20. We really value you and want to keep you (more promises, promises)

A team of employees work well together and are effective and productive under two bosses who enjoy sharing department leadership, and want to continue to work together if at all possible. The organization is undergoing restructuring with focus on excellence and productivity, and they are promised a larger working space/department as a reward for their productivity. Time passes and nothing happens. The larger office area never materializes. Company leaders continue to promise that such arrangements are in the works. One year goes by, then two years. The team begins to realize that the promises will never be realities. In the space of two years, they have seen other groups get exactly what they've been promised, and wonder why it hasn't happened to them. It finally dawns on them that the promises will never materialize and that this is the company's way of saying that it changed its mind and would rather that they leave (which turned out to be the true motive for the behavior). Eventually they do leave, but they never get any confirmation whatsoever that this was indeed the motive for the disrespectful and unprofessional treatment.

21. You didn't consult me and I don't like it

An employee makes the decision to spend a certain amount of money on one aspect of his project without consulting his boss, which is completely within his job description. For some reason, the boss finds fault with this particular decision, and without informing the employee as to the reason, removes him from the project and puts him on a less important project (essentially demotes him). This is all done without confrontation or communication of any kind. The boss never shows his anger overtly to the employee and the employee never receives a proper explanation. The employee later finds out that the reason he was 'demoted' was because he had made this decision without consulting his boss, even though he had previously made many such decisions before. Again, what is demoralizing about this situation is that the boss may have had other motives for demoting his employee, and that the real reason may have been something else completely, that the employee will never get to know. The passive-aggressive boss rarely is held accountable for his or her behavior towards his employees, and upper management will usually not question his or her decisions in the absence of a major explosion or rebellion.

22. Borderline behavior (but you'll never take me for it)

A male boss leads a small team that consists of both men and women, some young, some middle-aged. The women are for the most part independent thinkers and fairly strong-willed. The boss is a good deal older than most of the members on his team, and he is not very enamored of the independence he sees in the female members in particular. The younger women talk among themselves, compare notes and find out that the boss has made some inappropriate remarks to them during their meetings with him that have sexual overtones. He makes his comments in a joking manner, and he only does it in a one-to-one encounter, so that he can never really be taken for his comments. He also sits very close to them when he talks to them ('in their face' so to speak), and this too makes them feel uncomfortable. The same boss, in mixed-gender social situations, is fond of telling coarse sexual jokes, e.g. some of which have to do with fellatio, and these types of jokes make the women feel uncomfortable. Even the male group members find it uncomfortable, but attempts at trying to get the boss to stop talking like this are futile. The women agree that this is borderline behavior but know that there is little that can be done except to continue to confront him directly and say that they are not interested in such talk or behavior. They can walk away. But in some case the boss comes after them anyway to continue the conversation. What then? What are the motives for this behavior? It is intended to diminish and reduce the women to the sex objects that 'they should just know and accept that they are'. This behavior is also intended to punish women for thinking that they could in fact think of themselves as professional and worthy of respect. Women should know their place, according to these types of leaders. Over time it becomes clear that this leader really is a male chauvinist in the way he thinks about women and careers, and thus it really is no surprise that his attitudes are reflected in his speech and behavior. He may not want women to get ahead generally, he may be competing with one or several of them, or he may actually want some of them to leave his team and he tries to 'push' them out by behaving badly. Whatever the reason, his behavior is cowardly, dishonest and disrespectful, in other words, indirectly aggressive.

23. Let's keep the co-worker down (more stalling tactics)

An employee is waiting for valuable data from a co-worker so that he can finish a report he's working on. The co-worker keeps stalling and coming up with excuses for why he hasn't delivered the information. This goes on for several weeks, such that the report is overdue and the employee working on it begins to appear unprofessional to the boss. The co-worker who is stalling knows that this person is not going to tell the boss the real reason for the delay. This behavior is designed to trip up the person who is trying to get the job done correctly and well, and who is ambitious and wants to move ahead. This is one way of holding them back and making them look bad at the same time. It may even happen that the co-worker who is stalling suddenly comes up with the information at a time when the boss, who knows nothing about what has transpired, is present and can compliment this co-worker for his or her help and support on the project. In other words, the co-worker who stalled the project ends up looking like the good guy.

Two longer personal histories are included here to round out this chapter. Both histories depict passive-aggressive bosses and the power they have to destroy their employees. These stories will not completely explain why both bosses chose to behave in this way, but it is fairly obvious that both of them wanted to hang onto their power and control as best they could by sabotaging the chances their employees had to succeed. These bosses did succeed, but with different outcomes for the employees involved.

'Divide and Conquer'

This story demonstrates fairly typical passive-aggressive behavior on the part of a boss towards her employees, and may be the classical example of such behavior in many workplaces. A young woman in her twenties previously worked in an academic setting doing scientific research for several years for a woman who was known as a tough cookie. The student was young and relatively new to the field and was still feeling her way, learning about different work situations and people. Working for a tough woman didn't necessarily intimidate her. She figured she could learn a lot from this female boss about what it took to get to the top. It was difficult to find out who this female leader really was or how she actually treated her students prior to starting to work for her, since very few people in her group or at that particular department were willing to talk much about her. As it turned out, she had had quite a few problems with students in her group, as the student came to learn over time from former group members and co-workers at the department. The project on which the student was working was certainly interesting enough and she didn't have a problem generating data or presenting results to the group (she thought). However, it became apparent after about a year that nothing the student did was good enough for this boss. It didn't matter that she was spending a lot of time in the lab working. The student heard via others in the group, which consisted of mostly young women and several young men, that the boss was dissatisfied with her performance. She never said it directly to the student's face, but always behind her back. She criticized her not only to internal group members but to external co-workers and friends. Any chance she got, she talked disparagingly about the other members of her group to each person in the group when she got a hold of them. She was of course playing the same game with everyone in the group, a game known as 'divide and conquer'. If you succeed in setting each member in a group up against the other, you have complete control over those members with very little effort exerted on your part. Everyone outside of her group took what she said with a grain of salt, which was a small comfort at the very least, but of course you wondered how much of this kind of abuse your reputation could stand. The student considered it an odd way of behaving for a supposedly successful researcher. Why did she need to behave in this way if she was so secure and successful? Little did she know that many academic researchers (women and men both) exhibit some of the same characteristics that the student came to notice in her boss, an obsessive need for control, superficial friendliness and interest, lack of empathy, the ability to laugh at and cause others embarrassment under the guise of joking, especially if done in a public setting (you can almost get away with anything if you joke about it), and an annoying inability to make an informed decision and stick to it. Her boss could be very impulsive, both in making a decision to go down a particular path, and in deciding not to pursue that line of research anymore. She never bothered to inform her students about the reasons for her decisions. She could shift project focus mid-stream, such that the huge investment of time and money in that one particular project was wasted. Students simply had to accept her decisions and swallow their disappointment, anger, and frustration. There was a high employee turnover rate in that particular research group. Surprisingly, the group was productive in terms of publishing several articles per year in internationally well-known journals, a fact that most certainly attracted a continual flow of new students. How this was accomplished remains a mystery to the student to this day. She concluded that her boss was not stupid; she understood that in order to survive, she had to back off every now and then and give her students some leeway. Some projects had to get finished in order for the group to survive. She could compliment you when she wanted something from you, and those crumbs were enough to keep you going for a little while longer, such that you finished the work and eventually the project with her blessing (you were compliant).

The student tells her story so that others who are experiencing something similar will understand what they're up against. It is pointless to try to change this type of boss or work environment. Those working for her began to talk to each other and to understand that she treated the entire group badly. She had no favorites among them. The other group members told the student what she had said about her in the same way as the student eventually learned to tell them what she had said about them. They concluded that it was pointless to try to reason with her on an individual basis. In this way, they began to deal with her bad behavior as a united group, and it was the only way to deal with it. There was nothing to be gained by not telling the others in the group about how you felt and about what was happening. If you chose to deal with your problems in isolation, you were alone with your problems, your bitterness, your anger and your frustration.

The group did confront their boss on one occasion as a united unit, and that unity solved one particular problem that had bothered them. But of course they knew that they would have to do that for each problem that came along. So it was difficult to know if that was a feasible long-term solution, especially since most of them would be spending only three or four years in the group on the way to other jobs and studies. But it was a learning experience, and a valuable one, in that it taught the student that while it may have helped the situation generally if the academic leadership had learned about the dynamics in her group, it was more difficult to get up the nerve to actually inform them. Each of them in the group was unable or unwilling to go to the higher authorities so that something could be done about this boss, because to do so would have put them in the position of being a tattle-tale and whistle-blower and would have made it seem as though they couldn't take the heat. Everyone wants to give another person the benefit of the doubt, and no one thinks that it will be them who will have problems with the boss. That was the feeling that remained inside after years of mistreatment. The student figured if she just forgave one more transgression, the boss would eventually be nice and stop treating her badly. It never happened. The group should have gone as a united unit to the dean or provost and demanded help or action, but at the time, it seemed so impossible to think about doing it. Most of the people the student knew in the group at the time she was a part of it dealt with the boss by finding employment elsewhere, but most of them used three to four years to figure out exactly what was going on, their role in it, and that they could not solve it by dealing with her rationally. With no support from the highest leadership, who were either unaware of the situation or who turned a blind eye to it, there was no other recourse open to them. They had to quit. The student has the feeling that this is probably the most usual response to this type of behavior in a lot of organizations. And if the highest levels of management are filled with passive-aggressive individuals, they will never acknowledge the existence of this problem.

Punishing the employee for doing a good job

The following story has a darker outcome. A male employee in his mid-thirties worked for an older man who developed serious health problems. The employee was a hard worker who had been on the job a few years and had always had a cordial relationship with his boss, despite some misgivings about his qualifications as a leader. The boss was to be treated for a medical condition and he requested that the employee take over as leader for his team (with some reluctance) while he was away on sick leave. It is not clear whether this was suggested to the boss by his bosses or whether the employee's boss actually felt that he was the best man for the job. The employee said yes with some trepidation, but it worked out well enough and he saw it as an opportunity to learn and grow.

His boss was on medical leave for over a year, and the team functioned well under the employee. His leadership style was not heavy-handed, but rather more laid-back in contrast to his boss' style. He was not a control freak, was pleasant and professional in his dealings with his employees, and expected the position to be a temporary one. He was not the type to go after the boss's position. He did however get used to functioning independently and began slowly to reorganize and streamline projects, which he managed quite well. After one year, his boss returned to his old position and the employee welcomed him back without problems. Things seemed to return to normal. His boss acknowledged some of the changes and did not appear to be bothered by them. This is what the employee thought. Over the next year, he found out otherwise. Behind his back, his boss was talking negatively about him to other team members and to leaders in neighboring departments about the job the employee had done for him while he was away. It became clear to the employee that his boss resented that he had done such a good job taking care of the team while his boss was sick. The boss couldn't stand the fact that the employee was smarter and better with people than he was. The employee's co-workers came out in support of him initially, at least to his face. The situation became quite intense. The employee's boss ignored him for the most part and gave him little to no information about important work-related happenings. He never directly confronted the employee with his anger, resentment or dissatisfaction. This caused problems for the employee since he never felt he had enough substantial evidence to go to his boss with in order to talk to him about the unpleasant situation that had developed. His boss was never directly rude to him. But the more the employee found out about the negativity swirling around him, the more worried he became that his boss was trying to destroy him. He started to hear from co-workers that his boss was telling people that the employee was trying to take over his job. Finally the employee felt pushed into a corner and decided to write a letter to company management, which some of his co-workers signed, detailing the situation and presenting both sides. Both the employee and his boss were called into the director's office. The employee's boss denied that there was a problem and said that it was all in the employee's head. The co-workers who had originally signed the employee's letter refused to get further involved since they feared losing their jobs, so the employee was left alone to fight his fight. The situation got to the point where his boss informed the other team members that the employee was a traitor and that they were to have nothing to do with him. When the employee complained to management he did not receive any direct help. In fact, he found out later that management had chosen to side with his boss, for reasons that had more to do with cowardice and reluctance to deal with the situation. The employee had to resign his job and find employment elsewhere. His co-workers never did come to his defense again, and he felt that he left his job in disgrace. He distanced himself from that job and moved on, but the repercussions lasted for several years. He had to acknowledge his feelings of failure, his loss of self-esteem, his feelings of betrayal, his confusion over what had really happened, and ultimately, his powerlessness to do anything about the situation.

This is an extreme case of a passive-aggressive boss trying to destroy an employee. One could ask why the employee didn't just confront his boss early on with what he knew was going on, but of course the issue between them would have died then and there. His boss would have denied that anything was going on and the employee would have continued to feel powerless. His situation did not get better, and he ended up having to quit his job, but he did manage to get management to at least see that something odd was going on. Management chose to do nothing about it, but at least the employee registered his dissatisfaction about the dismal situation he was experiencing.

In the following chapters, I will discuss the emotional and psychological impact of passive-aggressive leadership on employees, describe some of the characteristics and personality traits that characterize employees who can be abused by passive-aggressive bosses, and finally discuss some of the possible ways of dealing with a passive-aggressive boss and work environment.

III

The emotional and psychological impact of passive-aggressive leadership on employees

The employees working for a passive-aggressive boss will initially be fooled by him or her, and even though they begin to understand what is going on after a certain amount of time, they continue to 'forgive' the boss his or her weaknesses, defend the boss and make him or her look good. I know employees who have been fooled many times into doing yet another project for the boss even though they already have enough to do or have been mistreated or taken advantage of several times before. Nevertheless, they help the boss because this response is also a consistent and learned response to years of passive-aggressive behavior on the boss' part. Such a boss may even be seen by company management as productive, but it is his or her employees who are making him or her look good by compensating for his or her weaknesses and unreliable behavior.

Over time, persistent passive-aggressive behavior on the part of leaders towards employees take their toll on hard-working, loyal employees. There are probably employees who are not unduly affected, but they are less interesting in the context of this book. Many hard-working loyal employees do suffer at the hands of a passive-aggressive boss. The puzzling aspect is that workplace productivity may not suffer immediately (if ever) due to the fact that the personality traits that characterize those individuals most affected by passive-aggressive leadership ensure that projects succeed rather than fail. I will present and discuss those traits in the next chapter. I do not for one second believe that the majority of employees want to view their bosses in a bad light. I do not believe that most employees are lazy, irresponsible, or disloyal, and I know for a fact that in all of the workplaces in which I have found myself, most employees were willing to give their all and more. Most wanted to work hard, do well, and make the company and their boss look good. I will grant that there are a minority of lazy passive workers who can cause their bosses a fair amount of aggravation. But most of the passive-aggressive behavior I have witnessed in the workplace has been in leadership and not in employees. I am often dismayed by the attitudes I have witnessed in company leadership when confronted with the problem of employee morale. It has not occurred to many leaders that perhaps their behavior has played a role in this problem. This is not surprising if they are passive-aggressive leaders, since they will lack the self-insight necessary to face themselves and make the necessary changes. As for the employees who must deal with these leaders on a daily basis, it may take a fair amount of time to figure out the dynamics of your work environment, to identify a passive-aggressive boss (or co-worker), and to figure out what is actually happening each time you have dealings with them. And still, once you have identified their behavior as passive-aggressive, it may not necessarily be any easier to cope with it or with how it makes you feel. It is how **you feel** after many years of passive-aggressive behavior that is the most important to understand.

How passive-aggressive leadership makes an employee feel

In the following section I will describe some of the ways you might end up feeling after being the recipient of passive-aggressive behavior for some years. Besides feeling an honest frustration and impatience at having to deal with the passive-aggressive behavior of leaders, you will end up questioning yourself nine times out of ten and wondering what you did wrong, or how communication could get so screwed up. You may also continually wonder why it is so impossible to set the situation right, to 'solve' (resolve) it once and for all. Here's how you might feel, and trust me, you may think you're imagining things, but you're not:

1. You've feel as though you've been blindsided and knocked off your center

This may be your first meeting with passive-aggressive behavior. You leave a meeting with your boss with the gut feeling that the meeting didn't go well (the reality is that the meeting didn't go well), and that your boss gained unhealthy control over you in an indirect way, but you cannot put your finger on how that happened. You cannot pinpoint the exact reasons for why you feel so lousy. Your boss didn't directly criticize your work (but he may have indirectly criticized you in some way), but perhaps a project you were working on was taken away from you or was ended abruptly without explanation. You have invested a lot of time in this project, and you ask why it's ending, but you get **no clear answer**. In fact, when you think back on it, you got **no response** to your question whatsoever. You **didn't anticipate** this outcome at all. You are told that you will be starting work on another project immediately, but you are **not told the reason why**. The whole meeting had an ambiguous tone to it. Your boss did all the talking, but you remember very little of what was actually said. There was no substance to the meeting other than that the outcome was that you were re-assigned to another project. You don't know exactly how to proceed from here and wait for instructions. You feel **let down, frustrated, angry**, but you have little recourse but to accept the boss' decision and start work on the new project. You tell yourself that the next time you'll do a better job, but still, something doesn't feel quite right because you know deep down that you did a great job on this project. You cannot put your finger on why all the alarm signals are sounding inside of you, but you do your best to ignore them and move on. This situation may repeat itself.

Sometimes it has to do with project leadership, other times it will have to do with your leadership being usurped by the boss midway through a project, while he insists that you are still the leader. Other such situations are finding out that other team members (your peers) are making more money than you are and are in fact doing less work, but they are 'yes men' to the boss and you are not.

2. You end up feeling that you are always wrong

No matter what you do, it seems that your way of thinking is incorrect and that you shouldn't think like that, because the boss says so. There's something **wrong with you** because you are ambitious or expect to be noticed or rewarded for a job well done. According to the boss, you should question your level of ambition and why you are so anxious to succeed, and you shouldn't think so much about the rewards, be they monetary or otherwise.

3. You feel as though you are being punished for something but cannot figure out the reason why

You are most likely being punished by the passive-aggressive boss because you call a spade a spade, are direct, honest, and assertive. You don't play the required political games. It's not winning you points with the boss and he 'punishes' you by not recommending you for a bonus/raise, for more challenging projects, or for project leadership.

4. You feel diminished, demoralized, lethargic and unfocused

You may feel depressed for no apparent reason, but deep down you're pretty sure it has something to do with how you're being treated at work. You begin to lose your self confidence and trust in yourself.

Everything feels negative. You feel as though you are being ignored, although again you cannot pinpoint exactly why or even how. The reality is that you ARE being ignored or passed over.

5. You feel duped and exploited

You get fooled time and again by the poseur, the actor-- whose feigned concern and interest, diplomatic manner, joviality and enthusiasm suddenly (re)appear in the boss when he wants something from you. You think he has changed, that this time he really is being a nice guy. However, once he has what he wants, namely your compliance, the sweet talk and nice guy approach are shelved. He is then free to ignore you until he has some new request of you, or free to make sarcastic comments about you or your work.

6. You are often the recipient of 'well-meaning' criticism

For example, your boss says you're not a team player, or you're not being helpful. Or you think only of yourself (you're selfish). The boss may even tell you that "you've changed" or "you are not as helpful as you used to be". You say no too often (reject others), according to the boss. Or you have emotional issues. And for some reason, when the boss says this initially, you believe it. After you hear it a few times, it may sink in that this is a tactic being used against you to make you more receptive or compliant to what the boss wants you to do, but nevertheless, it is an often effective tactic since it creates doubt in the employee about his or her behavior. When the passive-aggressive boss needs you to toe 'his' line, he makes these types of comments about you and knows you'll take it to heart, because that's what you've always done. And since an employee does want the boss to be pleased with his or her work performance, he or she will try very hard to accommodate the boss' wishes. If the employee reacts negatively to the criticism and tries to defend himself, he may find himself criticized for this as well ("you're too sensitive" or "you take everything so personally") or ending up trying to assuage the boss' feelings, who may react in a surprised way when confronted with his behavior ("only trying to help you or guide you"). The problem lies within yourself and you should change yourself, according to your boss.

7. You are the butt of the joke

The joke is always at your expense, if there is joking involved. You are the focus of the 'joke' or the sarcasm (and there is a lot of that), especially in front of other people who laugh along without understanding the dynamics that are really involved, because if they did, they wouldn't laugh. This is criticism under the guise of joking and sarcasm.

8. You begin to feel like you're losing your perception of reality

You begin to think that you are a crazy person because you are constantly wondering if you have heard things correctly or interpreted them correctly. You feel as though you've gotten sucked into a vortex of confusion and frustration. You wonder if what you are feeling is really true. How could it be so bad at work when everyone tells you how good you have it, or that you have such a nice, friendly boss? Other people (family and friends) say to you that it couldn't possibly be this bad, that you must be imagining things. You begin to feel paranoid and perhaps the boss even drops an offhand comment telling you that you are, especially when you try to discuss workplace problems directly.

9. You begin to feel an intense dislike of the passive-aggressive boss

You don't really want to be around him or her anymore. You begin to feel a kind of dread whenever you have to deal with that person. You'd like to avoid that person, but how can you, when that person is your boss?

10. You re-double your work efforts in an attempt to set the situation right

You think that more hard work will surely put you back in the passive-aggressive boss' good graces, but you end up right back where you were--problems with the boss, because you are dealing honestly whereas he or she is not.

If you can identify with several of these feelings in response to how you feel about yourself in your workplace, and how you feel about your work environment and your boss, you may be working for a passive-aggressive person. It takes you a while (possibly a few years) to figure out that you're not the only one in your workplace who feels this way or who is the recipient of this type of behavior. How you choose to deal with this fact will be a deciding factor for the quality of both your future work life and personal life. It is not unusual for feelings of work dissatisfaction to spill over into the home environment, with the expected results--arguing (if you are together with someone), depression, stress and anxiety. A man or woman who dreads going to work in the morning because he or she knows what awaits there, cannot just 'shut the door' on it at 5 pm, go home, and pretend that nothing bad happened during the day. Once you are aware of your situation, it becomes necessary to try to do something about it. And if you cannot do anything about it except be aware of the situation, that is still better than suffering with no awareness or understanding at all of why you are suffering.

IV

Employee beliefs and personality traits that
can be exploited by a passive-aggressive boss

You may have come to the point in your career where you just know intuitively that you are ready for the next step. From an objective point of view, you've done a good job, performed well, you know you are qualified, you know you have the ability to manage/lead a project and/or a team, and you know you can tackle the stress. You've done what your boss has asked you to do time and again, despite that some of those projects have been filled with difficulties and problems. Some of the projects have been nearly impossible to get done, and you've been direct with the boss about the problems and difficult situations that have arisen underway. You're solution-oriented, so you've tried to solve those problems yourself, but kept the boss informed of your protocols. On some occasions, you've actually said that the projects were not really feasible, but once you've stated your opinion, your boss disagrees and asks you to continue. You do. You've worked hard, worked overtime, sacrificed your home life when duty called, and made the boss look good when it counted. You know you're ambitious, smart, and that you like the challenges associated with new responsibilities and new positions. Nonetheless, you find that you are not advancing in your company. You don't know why. You talk to your boss in an honest and direct way about the situation, and he or she assures you that you have a future in the company, that things will change, and that soon it will be your turn to advance. He or she tells you to be patient and to wait. You wait, continue to make the boss look good, work hard, bide your time, and bank on the boss's words-- that next time it will be your turn. Next time comes. Someone else gets the promotion you wanted and worked for. Suddenly a few years have gone by. You're older, but still young enough to switch jobs if necessary. But you decide to wait until the next time around. Maybe the boss is right. Your turn is coming. The next time around comes and you are again bypassed. You begin to wonder what's wrong with you. That's the first thing you question. You don't start by wondering what's wrong with the boss or with company management generally. You instead wonder if the boss is disappointed in your performance, or doesn't think you're up to the job, or simply if he or she thinks you're not good enough. This, despite the fact that most other people you come into contact with, colleagues and friends alike, have told you for years that you're good enough, qualified enough, and that you deserve a promotion.

Employee beliefs and personality traits that can be exploited by a passive-aggressive leader

The fact that employees can be disappointed by their passive-aggressive boss and their work environment presupposes a certain philosophy that employees have that is the fundament of their work ethic and desire to be a good employee. Some of the beliefs and personality traits of employees who can be (and often are) exploited by a passive-aggressive boss (or co-worker) include:

- A strong work ethic is important. Working hard is a virtue. Do your best at all times.

- You'll be treated fairly in the workplace if you do a good job (life is ultimately fair). People generally treat each other fairly and honestly in the workplace. You will be rewarded for a job well-done (an 'unwritten' contract between you and your boss/company). If I do my job well, unpleasant things won't happen to me.

- *Feedback is important to you.* Constructive criticism, advice and praise concerning one's work results are necessary for you to function well in your job.

- *Loyalty is a virtue.* Leaders got to be leaders because they are smart and competent. They deserve their positions and are worthy of my respect and loyalty. Don't criticize the boss or your workplace. Don't engage in gossip about work or your boss because workplace gossip is not to be trusted.

- *Honesty is the best policy.* I should be honest and direct with others generally, and they will be honest with me. They will mostly say what they mean.

- *Persistence and stubbornness will pay off.* Stick with it, even if you run into problems. Don't be a quitter. It's better to win than to lose, but if you lose, don't be a sore loser. Swallow your pride.

- *Grin and bear it.* Don't complain. Be a positive and encouraging person in spite of the negativity around you. Forgive and forget. Don't hold a grudge. Don't be resentful or envious.

- *Try to solve problems* that arise without burdening the boss with them. Don't create problems where none exist. Don't bother the boss with the small things because he or she is a busy person.

- *Work politics don't really concern me.* I can get ahead without involving myself in them. It is best to be direct and not to play games. Playing games is not necessary to get ahead.

- *My opinion counts and will be respected.* However, when I disagree with the boss, the boss has the final say and his or her opinion should be respected.

An employee who has many of these strong beliefs may know at the bottom of his heart that they are not serving him well in his work environment, because he has witnessed enough unpleasant situations through the years or had them happen to him personally. He may not have gotten the promotion he was promised, for example. Or he may have seen that highly competent co-workers were bypassed for promotions or raises or treated unfairly for reasons he cannot figure out or understand. Nevertheless, he is tenacious in his beliefs. He doesn't really want to let go of them. It takes a long time and a lot of hard personal work to let go of beliefs and personality traits that don't 'fit' anymore. In truth, it is extremely unlikely that an employee will go from being a hard worker to being a slouch, or go from being a loyal employee to an anarchistic one, even if a person makes the decision to change. Most people simply don't shed their skins that quickly or at all. One reason may be that to consider the alternative scenarios, that, for example, life is mostly unfair, people are dishonest at heart, and loyalty is a waste of time and energy, so why should I be any different, are so negative and unpleasant that they are difficult to adopt. Such attitudes may be viewed as giving up, giving in, or as too excessive and extreme. Most people with beliefs in hard work, loyalty, justice and persistence have likely grown up in families that believed in the same, despite difficult realities that they lived with each day. They heard their parents talk about the workplace at the dinner table and they absorbed and learned by example. They watched fathers or mothers work long hours yet end up being bypassed for promotions and raises. They watched the same fathers or mothers swallow their pride and keep on working for the same companies despite being overlooked, underpaid, ignored, or mistreated, perhaps because they simply couldn't afford to quit and start over someplace else. Whatever the reasons, it is difficult to give up the idea that the world is fair and that leaders will behave logically and correctly once given the facts. It is hard to picture the opposite when starting out in the work world, and even after twenty or more years in the workforce, it can still be difficult to give up deep-rooted beliefs, essentially, that the world is a good and just place, and that the workplace will be the same. The ideas that 'this won't happen to me' or that 'it happened to others because of something they did that you are certain you will not do', are hard to relinquish.

The following story serves as a good example of the personality types that can be exploited by passive-aggressive bosses. A female employee in her early thirties worked for a passive-aggressive boss for a number of years before she did something about changing her job situation. Her view of the workplace changed considerably after many years of dealing with his passive-aggressive behavior. The desire to work was always one of the strongest motivating forces in this young woman for as long as she could remember. She cannot recall any point in her teenage and young adult life where she did not want to be a part of the work world. The desire to work and be a part of the work world stemmed from the many evenings she sat at the dinner table as a child, listening to her father talk about his day at the office. Although much of what he said was in fact critical of the corporate world, in terms of how meetings went and how decisions were made, he instilled in her the desire to be part of the team that was working for the good of the company. The prospect of being a full-time career woman was very attractive. One of the best compliments she can remember being paid as a young adult was that she had a **strong and admirable work ethic**. The compliment came from a woman she worked for as a teenager. The job was nothing more than a summer office job, but she poured her heart and soul into that job, just like she did into all the other summer jobs and part-time jobs that she has had. Looking back on it now, she realizes that the compliment revealed something about her that she was not conscious of at that time, namely that her work ethic came to her naturally; it was instinctive, visceral, from the gut. She doesn't remember having it 'taught' to her as so much else was. It just seemed right for her to **work hard and diligently**, to give a company its due and in return, it would treat you well.

She went on to college and then joined the workforce full-time after she graduated. She stayed only a few years in her first job, which was a very passive (and lackluster) work environment. Her second workplace was an assertive and constructive work environment. She consciously chose to work long hours in her new job. She was interested in gaining as much experience as possible, as it was an exciting, motivating, and dynamic work environment that respected its employees, and she was proud to work there. The job just kept evolving into something better and better. She began to travel to courses and conferences and to assume more responsibility and leadership. It was an unparalleled time in her life. She couldn't imagine any other life than that one. She loved working hard and she loved being a woman on her way up the career ladder. She loved the fact that the company she worked for trusted her to represent them at meetings and conferences. She loved the fact that she could travel on business and that the men she worked with respected the intelligence of the women with whom they worked. Her boss (and his boss again) were generous men, not afraid of dealing with women or supporting their career aspirations.

By the time she left her second job (she had gone as far as she could go there) she had doubled her starting salary, of which she was very proud. She took a new job in a different city. This new job proved to be the crucible that would test all her previously-held beliefs and feelings about the workplace generally. She worked long hours there also, including a lot of overtime and weekend work. Her evenings at home were often filled with extra work from the office, and her life quickly became defined by her job. However, she had flashes of misgivings here and there, without being able to directly pinpoint what the problem was. She knew something was wrong but she couldn't put her finger on what exactly. What she did know was that there was very little positive feedback from her work environment and from her boss concerning her projects and accomplishments. She mostly assumed that this was how things were done in this work environment, and that all work environments were bound to be different, so that she couldn't expect it to be like her previous work environment. Her boss was constantly coming into her office with new ideas and projects to take on. **Saying no was not initially an option**, even though she understood that he was unstructured, unfocused, disorganized and all over the board. His enthusiasm was such that she initially didn't have the heart to say no, because she too had enthusiasm of her own for many of the same ideas and potential projects. The difference between them was that he did not understand the logistics involved in taking on huge projects. She did because she was closer 'to the floor' so to speak, and was more structured and organized. He had no concept of what follow-through meant, which was an enormous responsibility for this employee who was not formally in charge of the team. She was given leadership tasks without having the formal title of leader, which may have worked fine in other workplaces but not in the one she found herself. She was **expected to plan, organize, strategize and follow through, but not to expect any rewards** (promotion) or compensation (higher salary or extra pay) for her hard work. This of course was never explicitly stated, but more implied through sarcastic and humorous comments about her ambitions and supposed greediness. The joke was always at her expense. It was always implied that she was too ambitious, too greedy, not a team player, that she just should accept her place and not aim much higher since that was the system she was dealing with. She was expected to be

compliant in all situations. She was often the recipient of an extremely irritating bravado that was ultimately demoralizing. "We" were going to do this or that (translated--his team, not him); "we" were going to show the others (translated--his team was going to make him look good), "we" were being treated unfairly (translated--someone else was always holding him back or keeping him down. He never even entertained the notion that maybe he was not quite good enough to be up there with the high fliers). She always felt uncomfortable at team meetings. Entire meetings could be spent discussing inane and banal issues rather than the work at hand. If she tried to get the discussion back on a professional track, it always veered off again on some other tangent that he wanted to discuss. If discussions arose about independent thinkers, individuals who went their own ways, the joke was always at her expense; it was implied that she was this kind of person and that it was not the best way to be. If she took a **serious professional approach** to a particular project, in terms of structuring and organizing it, it was always glossed over. He took the superficial approach and the rest of the team ended up compensating for his shortcomings. They made him look good, covered for him, and ignored his superficial Teflon approach as best they could. He would forget important decisions, forget what was discussed at previous meetings, and ignore the fact that he forgot them.

Many of her co-workers experienced the boss' behavior in much the same way as she did. They had worked there as long as she had and were pretty demoralized as well, which was moderately comforting to her in its own bizarre way. Since she was a **loyal worker** and one who hadn't, up to that point, challenged authority too much, she continued to try her best to please her boss and to accommodate his wishes and ideas. She did confront him from time to time about his unrealistic expectations in terms of the size of projects or their feasibility, or his inability to tackle problems that arose and which needed solutions. On those occasions, he would listen to her passively, quietly, and thank her for her input. She initially felt that he had 'heard' her on those occasions, but she came to understand that his passive reaction was the prelude to a more aggressive reaction that she never saw, but felt in different ways as time went on. He did not like being confronted, challenged, or questioned. Although it was never said explicitly, she and her co-workers came to understand that HE wanted to be the boss, despite his protests to the contrary. What he said directly was that he welcomed the input from his team. But this proved to be untrue time and again. Members of the team could go into his office and say the same thing that the employee had said to him about a project or a specific issue. He listened and then did exactly what he wanted, which resulted in his ignoring their suggestions for the most part. This young employee looked ahead and saw nothing except more hard work and very few rewards. Her salary was not increasing. She was continually overlooked for formal project leadership. She was still included in the actual working groups (translated = team members who actually do the hard, often menial work), such that she was 'rewarded' for her hard work with more hard work. She was good at organizing projects and because of her attention to detail, good at the follow-through that was required for the project to be successful. She was always asked to do more of the same. She had up to that point never done things at work purely to get the rewards that were presumably available (higher salary, better position, more leadership and responsibility), but mostly because she loved her work, but she began to wonder why after several years, nothing was really 'happening' for her in terms of job advancement. Every time she turned around, it was her boss who was getting noticed for the work that she had done or organized the team to get done; he was getting the salary increases, the prestige, and the leadership positions. She had been the same type of employee towards him that she had been towards her boss in her previous job. Whereas in her previous job the rewards were forthcoming, they were not in her present job. She began to rebel against the vision of herself as the loyal, predictable, reliable employee. She began to feel trapped by the stagnant view of herself, the confusing work environment, and the mixed signals she was getting all the time about her capabilities. The rewards also went to others who did much less than she did on projects. She began to feel a dislike of her job, of her work ethic, of herself. She felt that no one cared about her, the person she really was, and that she was slowly being lost, worn away. She felt overlooked and completely ignored, and became demoralized.

This employee now understands that her honest ambition and desire to do a good job were sabotaged. She understands that her loss of confidence in her abilities was the direct result of a passive-aggressive boss who did not like her direct approach, her honesty, her work ethic, her ambition, or her desire to do a thorough and complete job (pay attention to details and follow through). She believes now that her way of working pointed out to him his own shortcomings, and this he could not accept, so he had to push her off the path and keep her down. He felt threatened by her. He needed to find a way to punish her for being a better worker than he was. She also believes that passive-aggressive people are basically lazy. They take short cuts if they can find them. They cut corners when they need to or want to, over the objections or protests of others, but they reap the rewards for others' hard work. They tend to prefer others who think the way they do (and in her case, her boss preferred his male employees), so that other team members who think like the boss are preferred, promoted, and also encouraged to take the (many) short cuts that exist on the way to the top and to find others who are willing to do the brunt of the hard work for them. She did not want to believe that the workplace functioned in this way. She thought it was just this particular work environment that functioned this way, since it hadn't been like this in her previous workplace. She held onto that earlier work experience for all it was worth--a workplace where hard work, honest ambition and direct assertive communication between boss and employee were rewarded. She understands now, after many years of self-ransacking and workplace analysis that it does not bother her for a second that a decent hard-working respectful boss would reap the rewards for his or her hard work as long as he had taken the job seriously, respected his or her employees, and rewarded them as much as he or she rewarded themselves. But for a long time, and especially when she was down on herself, she concluded that she was an envious, paranoid, and negative person and that she was not fit for the work she was doing. For most of her adult life, she had **believed in the value of hard work** for herself and women generally. She believes strongly that women should have their own incomes, their own careers and the resulting independence that comes from that. She has become a person who now struggles daily with the idea that much of what she was taught was a lie, designed to make women accept their (often low-level) status in the work world. We cannot all be chiefs, so we must learn to be Indians. This is something she has been told many times by this same boss.

So what are the **mixed messages and signals** that she received from her boss on a regular basis? She was told that she could function as a leader, since she was given the responsibilities and tasks of a leader, which she then accomplished in a satisfactory manner (efficient, timely, and productive). She was then told that she thought too highly of herself, that she worked too hard, that her standards were too high, that she wasn't a team player, that she could be negative or rejecting or aggressive, or that she was too independent (admonished by her boss for 'trying' to be a leader). She was told many things that were all presented to her in front of other team members in a joking fashion. No matter what she did, there was always something which was commented upon or criticized in a 'well-meaning' way. It was not possible for him to ever say in a serious way that she had done a great job, or that he was proud of her and the team members (whom she had organized) who had worked so hard on this or that project. It occurs to her now many years later that he never said that he was proud of any work produced by his team. All achievements were just ignored in the race to start on the next great project that was going to make him famous or grab him a lot of attention.

Although she no longer works for this person, she understands the damage that was done. It is insidious, the type of damage a passive-aggressive boss will inflict on employees. Slowly, over time, passive-aggressive bosses wear employees down. Passive-aggressive behavior whittles away their self-confidence, focus, clarity, enthusiasm, willingness to help others, and patience. Enough becomes enough, and the frustration involved in dealing with a passive-aggressive boss eventually becomes the deciding factor in wanting to leave the job. This employee wanted to quit her job many times, but she always found reasons to stay. She ended up staying too long. Why? There are many reasons. **The team needed her.** She **put their wishes ahead of her own.** She liked the actual work she was doing. She enjoyed the projects she was working on as long as she didn't have to deal with her boss on a daily basis, which she didn't have to. It took her a long time to understand the dynamics of the relationship between her and her boss. The time it took to understand these work dynamics is probably the major reason she stayed so long in the job. It did not take her very long in a new job to understand or recognize passive-aggressive behavior when she saw it. So this is one of the positive things that came out of a rather negative experience. She can also recognize it when other people she knows, be they friends or family, talk to her about their work situations and describe themselves as demoralized, frustrated, confused, or unsure about their capabilities. She sees the value of honest communication and she also sees how difficult it is to achieve that, and how difficult it is to be a good leader.

How did she bypass her fear and muster the strength and courage to shift jobs? She learned first how to detach from her work situation, but only after several years of trying and failing. How did she manage to detach from her work situation? She began with simple things, such as giving up carrying a full briefcase with unfinished work home with her each night. Sitting at home each evening and not finishing up work had always made her feel guilty. So coming home with an empty briefcase helped. She also tried to talk less about work and more about other things that interested her. She slowly developed new interests and hobbies, which helped reduce the elevated position work and some work-related problems had assumed in her life. She now goes home at a decent hour, despite the internal protests of 'not being finished'. She realized that her work will never really be finished, since there are always new and more projects to do. She knows that she swallowed the concept of overwork without questioning it at all, without questioning the effect on family, health (physical and psychological), and friendships. She has also come to realize that life is short. As Anna Quindlen wrote in A Short Guide to a Happy Life, "No man ever said on his deathbed I wish I had spent more time at the office" (3). She now thinks that statement says it all. She is currently in a new job, is enjoying it, but knows when to go home and leave it behind. She is still interested in her field, but knows her limits. She also knows passive aggression when she sees it, and tries to stay out of the path of passive-aggressive individuals as much as is reasonably possible. If she has to deal with them, she tries to stay focused and to write down what transpired in meetings with them in order to be prepared for the future confusing and frustrating scenarios that she knows will occur. She tries to remain emotionally-detached from her workplace so that she can remain objective about it. So far, she feels it is working out for her but never entirely rules out the possibility that she could be blindsided at some future point.

V
Fighting back - Survive and thrive by being more assertive

Why should passive-aggressive behavior in workplace leadership be treated as a serious problem? The answer is simple. Passive-aggressive bosses can destroy the morale of their employees. Over time, demoralized employees will work less, produce less, and care less. This will mean reduced work output and reduced efficiency. But this may not happen immediately, and in some work environments it may never happen, for reasons that I have described previously. The question is why passive-aggressive leadership is tolerated in a work environment at all. That is a more difficult question to answer. The simplest answer is that company management is reluctant to act unless actively pressured to do so. If the company is reasonably productive, why rock the boat? Why look for trouble where there is none? Why make a mountain out of a molehill? If no one (translated--one or more employees) is complaining then there is no problem. The real concern is why employees do not complain more about their work situation if it borders on intolerable. Why don't more employees fight back rather than accept inappropriate behavior? The majority of employees often adopt a 'grin and bear it' attitude when problems arise at work. Many of them believe (perhaps incorrectly) that management won't really do anything about a problem if they complain, or will shove the problem under the rug and pretend it doesn't exist. Many workers have been brought up to believe that you just accept your lot in life. You are so often told that "others are worse off than you are". "You at least have a job. What are you complaining about?" Employees, who voice complaints, while their grievances may be real problems, are often viewed as negative and irritating individuals, as tattle-tales, or as whistle-blowers, and such employees are often not taken seriously. Company management may have a hard time acknowledging the existence of real problems, and I can imagine that to acknowledge that one of their own has passive-aggressive behavior issues that are impacting negatively on employee morale makes them want to run for cover. It may be easier for an organization to label the employee as difficult and to eventually get rid of that person rather than getting rid of the boss. And if the passive-aggressive problem is systemic, then an employee may find himself in a very tough situation if he decides to fight it. But it may be worth it in the end, even if the result is that you end up switching jobs. It may be worth fighting back so that you recover your self-esteem and confidence and let your boss know that you are not going to take the abuse anymore.

Some solutions for dealing with a passive-aggressive boss/workplace

Once you as the employee understand that the frustration and craziness that you are experiencing at work are the result of passive-aggressive leadership, you can begin to understand your role in the dance between you and your boss (misplaced loyalty, outdated beliefs) and your chances of tackling the problem you face. We are not talking about necessarily changing the boss' behavior, but about changing your behavior, which may be difficult but not impossible. It may be difficult because many of your responses to your current workplace are 'programmed' inside you already. Awareness of this is the key to starting to fight back.

There are viable tactics and solutions to dealing with a passive-aggressive boss or a passive-aggressive work environment, and these are presented in the following sections.

1. Start by detaching from your work environment.

This is very hard to do initially when you are in the midst of craziness that you do not understand. But try to do it. Try to step back from your daily work situation. Slow yourself down mentally; try to relax your mind in order to be able to observe and to dissect the dynamics of your work environment. If you can detach from your work situation to any degree, it will help you to think objectively about it. Use some time to identify what you consider to be the major problems in the workplace. Also do the math--if you are spending more time each day trying to figure out workplace dynamics and less time on actual work projects, you have a major problem. Try to figure out whether passive-aggressive behavior is the major problem, and work from there.

2. Make a list of pros and cons

Put down on paper what you like and don't like about your job or boss, your strengths and weaknesses in that environment, and what is perceived to be true and false about your work environment. Include how you feel about your work situation at any given time. It helps to have some self-insight, but you can ask others whom you trust for help, as well as your co-workers. You should ask someone you know will discuss your strengths and weaknesses in work-related areas with you in a serious manner. Write it and put it away for a few months, and then take it out again, look at it and see if you still feel the same way about your job. One co-worker I know did just that--he wrote a list of pros and cons at a time when he understood that it was time to move on from his job to get away from his passive-aggressive boss. He had exhausted all possibilities for dealing with her and nothing had worked. His advancement was blocked at all turns, and he was completely demoralized. He wrote the list and put it away for six months, and then took it out again and read it. It allowed him to sum up and assess his job situation, and he ultimately saw that nothing had changed in the six-month time period, despite repeated conversations with his boss about his career ambitions. His 'hope' that things would change proved to be fruitless. In his case, writing the list proved to be very helpful in making the decision to shift jobs. He found another job that gave him the possibility of career advancement, but only after making sure that his new boss was someone with whom he felt comfortable. He looked for some telltale behavior--joking, irony, superficiality--that would have indicated possible problems that he wished to avoid in a new job.

3. Understand that dishonesty is the crux of the passive-aggressive behavior problem.

Passive-aggressive people are dishonest, and a passive-aggressive work environment is dishonest and full of mixed signals. Think about some of the following questions. Why do employees who work for a passive-aggressive boss end up feeling frustrated and demoralized only gradually? Why don't employees recognize a passive-aggressive boss immediately? You need to see the overall pattern in passive-aggressive behavior. It is a persistent pattern of dishonesty, deceit, negativity, and ambiguity, and it takes time to recognize and to understand this. Don't feel bad because it took you a few years to understand what was going on. Try to see that this negativistic pattern of behavior is designed to bring you down and make you feel small. And once your self-confidence is negligible, you are easier to control.

4. Don't let depression and negativity defeat you.

Don't succumb to hopelessness. You may feel that you have no outlet for your anger at your passive-aggressive boss. You have tried to discuss issues or problems with a passive-aggressive boss and have been told that you are imagining things, not to take yourself too seriously, to relax because it cannot be that bad, that you are off balance, having a bad day or worse still, that he or she understands your concerns. Nothing changes and the abuse continues. As long as you do nothing, nothing will change. The boss sees no reason for change as long as you accept his or her reluctance to do something positive about the situation. The employee who works for a passive-aggressive boss must understand this if he or she decides to fight the tactics being used against him or her. Remember that you do in fact have an outlet for your anger and that you don't have to become passive-aggressive yourself in order to survive and thrive. Some people choose to become passive-aggressive like their bosses in order to get ahead, and workplace dynamics merely perpetuate themselves. For example, an employee's unresolved anger may find an outlet in behavior that leads to project sabotage. An aggressive work environment may seem preferable at times, if only because at least with (a certain level of) aggression, you know where you have people, where they stand, whether or not they like you, or whether they like your work. You may feel attacked at times, but at least you know when you are being attacked and you can defend yourself immediately. Overall however, an assertive work environment is the most constructive type of work environment. I know of assertive work environments that respect their employees. They function well and they lead to employee satisfaction. These should be the goals--satisfied employees and a productive work environment. Assertiveness implies being honest, direct, opening up, talking, communicating, and making a real effort to deal with problems by facing them head-on. If this is discouraged in a workplace, then its employees are trapped in a living hell. If a workplace cannot admit that there are real problems that are causing employees a lot of grief, then that workplace will be ensnared indefinitely with those problems, with no hope of change. The reluctance to open up will lead to remoteness, complacency, cynicism, fatalism and ultimately to ineffectiveness.

5. Set boundaries that you don't want others to cross and verbalize them to your passive-aggressive boss.

This is the shrewd approach to dealing with any workplace you find yourself in. It may sound obvious, but in my experience very few colleagues have actually thought this through thoroughly, and they end up frustrated time and again because they fell into the same trap--they didn't establish boundaries or they waited for others to establish boundaries for them. Verbalize your boundaries to yourself first so that you internalize them. Practice makes perfect. Visualize yourself saying no when you mean no, or confronting your boss on his behavior. Make sure you remind yourself about your boundaries daily. Then verbalize your boundaries to your boss as often as is necessary. If you don't do this, your passive-aggressive boss will exploit your inability set boundaries. You also need to know precisely what you will accept in terms of borderline behavior so that you are prepared to report your boss if he or she steps over the line. No one should have to accept abuse at work as part of their job.

6. Be assertive and find your voice.

Assertiveness is the key to changing your response to a dysfunctional work environment, not aggression, passivity, or passive-aggression. The importance of learning to speak up in an honest and direct way cannot be overemphasized. Remember, the passive-aggressive work environment has had a marked and demoralizing effect upon you, especially the longer you have been a part of it. Working for a leader who demoralizes you functions for that leader but not for you.

Remember that no one in power behaves in a way that will strip them of that power. Leaders who are obsessed with power and control will want to hold onto their power and control over others. Getting your self-confidence back will not happen overnight. Finding your voice and learning to be assertive will not happen overnight. But they will happen if you start by living one day at a time and by dealing with one unpleasant situation at a time. If you stand up for yourself once a week in the beginning, it's better than never standing up for yourself at all. Standing up for yourself and saying "I don't need or want to tolerate this particular behavior or comment from you anymore" IS an option. If the boss doesn't like it, he or she may fire you, demote you or simply ignore you (and the latter is what you've been dealing with anyway). So why not fight back? The importance of self-respect, respecting others, and standing up for yourself in an assertive way will help change *some crucial* aspects of your work situation. It may not make you well-liked, but that is not the major concern. Make an attempt to say "No, I don't want to do it that way" when you mean it. Say no to projects that will overwhelm you. If you are confronted with a bizarre comment from your passive-aggressive boss, ask him or her to repeat what they said. This is actually quite effective, since it gives you the confirmation you need that what was just said to you was inappropriate, and you may find that your boss is suddenly hemming and hawing and is reluctant to repeat himself. Make sure you let others know about what just transpired. Let others know what the boss has said to you. Don't create, participate in, or perpetuate an environment of secrecy that protects your boss. You may be embarrassed or bewildered by the boss's behavior, but it is only by opening your mouth and talking to other co-workers about it that you educate them about your boss and perhaps even find out that others have had the same experience with him or her.

Withdraw from projects that are draining your talents and energy and for which you get no credit. Learn about your workplace and who the company managers are. Go over your boss' head and inform upper management that you exist. Do it by email if you feel strange about doing it in person, but inform them of who you are. Inform them about your project ideas (especially if you have a boss who always tries to take credit for them), your contributions to specific projects and your achievements. Send copies of these emails to your boss and to yourself so you have a record of your communications. Make sure you do this all the time when you have come up with ideas for which you know your boss will take credit. Your passive-aggressive boss may not like this approach, but keep at it. The more people know about you, your suggestions and ideas, and your work, the better. You are fighting back, and it is necessary if you want to deal with your current situation, especially if you know that confronting your boss directly has had no long-lasting effect when you've tried it. Try not to behave in a passive-aggressive manner yourself. After years of passive-aggressive treatment you may have concluded that you need to behave passive-aggressively in order to survive, and you may already be treating others this way, because if "you can't beat them, join them". This is the insidious nature of the passive-aggressive work environment--it perpetuates itself and creates real possibilities for project sabotage and long-lasting damage.

7. Get an expert on your side.

If you are experiencing abuse at the hands of a passive-aggressive boss, talk about your situation with a therapist, a coach, a human resources contact, or a union official. This might be the push you need to find your voice and to become more assertive. They can help you. Verbalizing your 'secrets' and bringing things out into the open is a positive step and will give you the confidence to go further. When you know you have support and someone on your side, go right to the top--to company management. It may help your situation and you may be surprised by what you find out. For example, a female student was treated poorly over a long time period by her passive-aggressive female boss, who derided her work in front of her peers in the group during meetings in a snide and mocking way. She also was fond of sarcastically commenting on the lack of work ethic that this student had, which was strange to say the least because this student put in long hours and worked weekends and a lot of overtime, and everyone else in the group knew this. This student was given very difficult projects to accomplish, with little to no help or supervision, and was expected to master the intellectual and technical aspects of the projects without the boss' involvement. This was a tactic that the boss used against this student because she didn't like her and she didn't want her to succeed. The boss felt that she was too assertive and that she opened her mouth too much to tell the boss that this or that aspect of the project was not working or was not feasible. She essentially told her boss that the projects were not well-thought out, which they were not. She criticized the boss, in other words, but not in a rude way, simply in an honest way, but the boss took it personally. Eventually this student got tired of being abused and went to the director of the institute, and a meeting to discuss the situation was arranged between the student and her boss with members of the administration present. The student did the right thing by getting her superiors involved. The student had the guts to confront her boss and to fight back. What the student wanted was a boss who would help her finish her doctoral degree, as that was the (signed) contract between them. They do not have to like each other, but the student has a right to guidance and supervision. What the student did find out was that several previous students had also gone to the top to complain about this boss. Resolution of these types of personnel conflicts does not necessarily mean that both parties will end up liking each other, but they may end up respecting each other, however grudgingly. This has to be understood as well. If company management won't (or can't) help you, then it may be time to consider your legal options. You can report your company to the relevant authorities/officials that deal with worker grievances so that they can take on your case.

8. You may find a better and more supportive workplace if you switch jobs.

If all your attempts at trying to deal with your passive-aggressive boss fail, remember that not all leaders and workplaces are the same. Some situations may be so bad that it may be smarter to find a new job rather than try to deal with the dynamics of your current workplace, especially if the passive-aggressiveness is systemic and you find yourself blocked at all turns. This means that company management is part of the problem and that they cannot be counted on to help you. The quality of your life should be the major focus. The major concerns should be how you feel about yourself and if you are able to survive in a dismal, possibly harmful work environment. If you find that your work ethics and personal ethics are being compromised on a daily basis, if you are feeling that it is better to become a passive-aggressive individual yourself in order to survive, it may be time to quit and find a new job. If you do decide to leave your present job, make sure that you prepare a written summary of your work experience that you can submit to company management. Explain the problems you encountered at that workplace and make sure management knows in clear language the reasons you quit.

9. Have a good balance between your work life and your personal life.

It is neither productive nor smart to devote all your time to working at the expense of everything else in your life: family, friends, hobbies, interests, and so forth. Don't allow your work situation to become an obsession. If it has become an obsession, make a conscious effort to deal with it. Sometimes it ends up being all an employee can talk about, and family members and friends may be tired of listening to the employee complain, or frustrated themselves by their inability to help. Start by admitting you have a problem. Or seek professional help in the form of therapy or counseling if you feel that you cannot deal with it alone. It takes time to cut the cord connecting you to your job situation, but with a concerted effort over time, it will happen. There is life outside of work. Your job does not and should not solely define who you are.

10. Before starting a new job, find out all you can about where you will be working.

Pay attention to your gut feelings. During your interviews, keep your eyes and ears open. Your gut feelings about a workplace may be right on target. You can identify a closed, silent, sullen and negative work environment as well as an open, social and positive one. You just have to pay close attention to details. Once you start a new job, be a people person without being a gossip. Observe how leaders interact with each other generally and with their employees. Observe how the workplace treats both men and women. Is there respect for all employees, and not just male employees? You should be able to find this out relatively quickly. Observe whether women are advancing or if they are continually passed over in favor of men for leadership positions. At present, in most workplaces, men still hold the majority of leadership positions. The existence of the 'glass ceiling' is a problem for women in many workplaces and may be compounded by the existence of passive-aggressive behavior in (predominantly male) leaders.

11. What companies can do to make their workplaces thrive.

Companies can take concrete steps to deal with problems that have to do with suboptimal employee morale and with passive-aggressive bosses once they become aware of them. If employees report problems to management, it should be a given that management takes these problems seriously and tries to solve the conflicts. Management should not automatically side with its own.

Companies should not be afraid to get rid of managers who cause problems for employees, especially once they are aware that these managers are behaving in passive-aggressive manners towards employees and making their lives miserable. They should not be afraid to do something about the situation and should not just ignore it in favor of preserving the status quo. Real communication takes work. Both partners have to be willing to communicate honestly. This means that an employee has the responsibility to report a work problem in the same way that his boss has the responsibility to listen to that employee and to acknowledge that there is a problem and to try to seriously do something to solve it. The best solution may be to involve management consultants and conflict resolution experts who focus on detoxifying negative work environments if that will change things for the better.

Leaders should focus on improving their emotional intelligence and listening capabilities. This can be done through leadership courses that emphasize emotional intelligence (EQ) and conflict resolution. Individuals often become managers without the necessary qualifications for leadership. Leadership qualities are often not evaluated correctly when a person is being considered for a leadership position. Necessary qualifications should include a high EQ, the ability to listen well and to communicate directly and assertively, the ability to focus and to organize, and the ability to make decisions (in addition to being highly-competent). The ability to listen well is not the same thing as listening to employees complain incessantly. It means listening carefully and seriously to what an employee has to say and then repeating back to the employee the gist of what the employee communicated in a non-joking, non-sarcastic manner. In this way, the employee knows that he has been taken seriously. An employee may function better if he knows that at least the boss is aware of a problem even if it doesn't get solved right away. Managers have to and can learn to communicate with their employees in a direct, rational, honest, way, especially if they are deficient in these areas. If you are a boss, make a wholehearted decision to think about your behavior. Take a long hard look at yourself and try to be honest and objective. If you know deep down that your employees don't really respect you, you have to ask yourself why. It may be because you are not competent enough, but more likely it is because you do not treat your employees with the respect they deserve. Examine your behavior for passive-aggressive tendencies and traits. Eliminate sarcasm and joking from your interactions with employees and co-workers. You CAN change and your employees will notice the changes. A high level of employee satisfaction in the workplace is the direct result of leaders who possess high levels of emotional intelligence as well as high levels of competence. This cannot be overemphasized in modern work environments that often prioritize high levels of competence to the exclusion of all else.

Some questions and considerations: cultural influences and different types of workplaces

Some questions that you may want to think about are as follows: Is overt aggressiveness or pure passivity rewarded in the workplace generally? The answer is usually no, because overtly aggressive leadership can immediately destroy employee morale and effectiveness whereas passive leadership does not inspire efficiency or enthusiasm. Is passive-aggressive leadership rewarded in the workplace? Is the passive-aggressive boss aware of what he or she is doing? How is it possible that they are not aware? Do passive-aggressive leaders understand that they are rewarded for their behavior? A passive-aggressive boss is rewarded by his work environment. That is my conclusion after many years in the workforce. There are clear advantages to having leaders in a company who don't show anger (are not overtly aggressive) but who can 'get the job done' (translated, be ruthless in a devious but silent way = passive-aggressive). Such behavior is rewarded—if nothing was to be gained from being passive-aggressive, smart people would not choose to behave in this manner.

Are teasing, sarcasm, joking, innuendo and veiled comments forms of passive-aggressive behavior? In my opinion they are. A boss who jokes about an employee's personality traits and ambitions or is sarcastic about an employee's work on a particular project is behaving in a passive-aggressive manner. There is obviously something about the employee that the boss is uncomfortable with or doesn't like, or perhaps the boss thinks that the employee could have done a better job on the project, but the passive-aggressive boss will not confront the employee directly. The work environment should be about professional, honest and respectful behavior on the part of leaders towards employees, and vice versa. Some people will say, "Oh, it's only a joke, don't take it so seriously". Or you may hear that you have no sense of humor. But joking always has undercurrents of seriousness, and you need to pay attention to the types of jokes, the innuendo, as well as to who is telling the joke and the response of the workplace to that person. There is also no room for any type of sexually harassing behavior in the workplace. Teasing, joking, innuendo and veiled comments can also be forms of sexual harassment, depending on who is doing it, the recipients involved, and the motives involved. A boss should not be engaging in this type of behavior towards his or her employees, because this behavior only serves to confuse the recipients (mixed signals). Employees may think the boss likes them and are pleased by that, at the same time that their gut feelings tell them that the boss has crossed over a boundary that they wish deep down had not been crossed. Overall, such borderline behavior only serves to make employees 'feel' the unequal balance of power between themselves and the boss, and that may be the overall point. It is a way of keeping women (and men) down. It's a way of making employees feel 'small'. The boss can 'get away' with this type of behavior simply because he or she is the boss. Generally, a male boss should never give mixed signals to his female employees. He should be clear about where he stands and should be professional, focused, direct and supportive of them. Female employees should feel supported, secure and unafraid around him. The same should hold for male employees who work for a female boss. If borderline sexually harassing behavior is part of workplace dynamics, you will need to understand what it is about before you attempt to deal with it or to fight it. The question should not be why a woman or man feels uncomfortable listening to a coarse off-color joke, but why this type of joke is being told at all in a mixed-gender workplace. What is the real reason for telling it? What is it meant to accomplish, and why is it funny? Most men who behave towards women in this way in the workplace are insecure men with low levels of self-esteem, and many of the characteristics that define passive-aggressive people could be applied to them. They lack self-insight and emotional intelligence. If they had these, they would understand how their behavior is hurtful to the women who work for them. Nevertheless, these deficiencies do not excuse their behavior, and employees have every right to stand up to this behavior, to confront their boss on his or her behavior, and to demand an end to it.

It is also important to consider that there may be cultural differences that play a role in workplace dynamics. For example, the cultural reserve in Scandinavia may contribute to passive-aggressive leadership in workplaces because there is often a hesitation or a resistance to complaining publicly or openly, to attracting attention to oneself or to delving too deeply into another person's life or problems. This reserve has advantages and disadvantages. It protects one from an invasion of privacy, but it also hinders open discussions of real problems, which can spell major problems for dysfunctional workplaces. If you have problems with your boss at work, you can end up feeling that you must solve them on your own. Asking for help or getting others involved is not often encouraged. If you complain, it is often met with a 'that's the way life is' sort of attitude, and you end up feeling as though there may not be much to do about the situation, or that you were foolish to have brought up the problem at all. Additionally, there often is not much to do about a job you don't like or with which you are dissatisfied, because there are fewer alternatives than in the USA if you want to switch jobs, for example. This means that you often learn to (or are expected to) 'grin and bear it', i.e. be stoic about your situation, but the emotional and psychological costs of doing so may be quite high. There may be little to be gained by complaining, because the passive-aggressive behavior in your workplace may be so entrenched that you know before you open your mouth that it's futile to try to change your work environment. So you don't try. You stick with it and hope for the best. But you see that it is sometimes so unpleasant that some people just cannot take it anymore and they quit, or leave their professions and do something else in the hope of changing their lives.

Additionally, even within the same country, there will be different types of boss-employee relationships and workplace dynamics. Different companies will have diverse ideas about how bosses and employees should relate, and this may vary from state to state, from coast to coast, and from company to company. Whether or not a passive-aggressive workplace can be changed for the better may depend on the hierarchy and structure within each organization. Some organizations are more traditionally hierarchical than others, with a strong leader at the top, and a small number of project leaders who report to him or her. Other work environments are more 'democratic', with emphasis on shared leadership. The latter may actually contribute to better relationships, since leaders who know that they are to share power and positions might have a better chance at trying to share that power fairly, and this may benefit their employees. However, a traditional hierarchical work environment, with one main leader who supervises other team leaders, can also function well if that leader has the qualities of a good leader. For example, I have witnessed workplaces in Norway and in the USA with one strong leader where employees felt valued and respected, as well as workplaces with shared leadership that created a high level of employee dissatisfaction. The latter did not work because the leaders involved did not acknowledge the existence of passive-aggressive behavior in any one of them, such that the end result was merely confusion, frustration, and dissatisfaction in their employees. I don't have statistical documentation to support whether the one or the other leadership structure is better for a work environment. I have seen both types of structures function well in terms of creating an environment where employees felt valued, and I have also seen both of these organizational structures lead to dysfunctional work environments.

Another question is whether passive-aggressive leadership flourishes better in academic settings or in corporate ones. If the stories I have heard from different colleagues and friends who work in corporate settings are any indication, passive-aggressive leadership is not unique to academia. But if it flourishes better in academic environments, it may be because academia encourages cutthroat competition for power and prestige with its 'publish or perish' mentality, and some individuals who want to make it to the top will use all means necessary, including keeping others down, as a way of getting to the top, and once at the top, for retaining control. But since you may be 'stuck' with your employees or co-workers for many years, especially if you get tenure, the passive-aggressive approach to getting ahead may serve you better than the purely aggressive approach. For example, a principal investigator who has gotten to the top after years of struggle and who now leads a research group may be quite unwilling to relinquish his or her power and control when it comes to dealing with the people (students and scientists) who work for him or her. He (or she) may be an insecure group leader, unsure of his or her competence, or he or she may actually fear the intelligence of some of his or her students and research personnel. He or she may keep employees down by using passive-aggressive behavior to sabotage employees' efforts to get ahead, to advance up the career ladder, to publish papers, and to get research grants that will make them independent scientists in their own right, but all of this behavior will always be 'right on the border' of what is unacceptable. There will always be excuses for the behavior, or a perplexed response from the boss as to why the employee thinks that he is being bypassed, ignored, or held down. Why do academic leaders behave in this way? If those students and junior scientists realize how qualified they are, they will want to move on (and possibly even compete with their former boss for research funding) and then the boss' power and prestige will be diminished. It seems like such an immature (and counter-productive) way to behave, given the fact that the function of academia is to educate students who will eventually assume the same roles that current leaders have now. If you understand yourself and the meaning of your life, you know that you cannot stop the flow of progress, change, or most importantly, the aging process. You will get old one day and you will have to retire (or be forced out). Someone will eventually replace you. The best thing to do therefore is to try to be a competent leader once you've reached that level, and to be a good boss who encourages his or her team members to do the best they can, to succeed, and to become independent thinkers and group leaders. Many leaders fall short of this ideal.

Epilogue

Passive-aggressive behavior as practiced by any or all levels of management only serves to create mixed signals, confusion, frustration, anger and hopelessness in employees. The question is how will employees working for passive-aggressive leaders deal with their workplace and their bosses once they recognize their behavior for what it is. I have worked primarily in academic settings for most of my professional life, and have witnessed as well as experienced passive-aggressive leadership, but also good leadership. It is possible to thrive given an assertive and functioning work environment that prioritizes employee satisfaction.

I hope that this book has helped to open your eyes to the problem of passive-aggressive leadership in the workplace, and that you are now able to recognize a passive-aggressive work environment for what it is--dishonest and indirectly aggressive. Suboptimal, frustrating work environments are not solely the result of problematic employee behavior. I believe that employees react to their leadership. Assertive and constructive leadership will have a positive and encouraging effect on employees. Passive-aggressive leadership will have a damaging effect on employees and on work environments generally, and may end up creating a whole new generation of future passive-aggressive leaders. This should be discouraged at all costs. My hope is that companies with employee morale problems and high personnel turnover rates will take a long hard look at how their leaders behave towards employees, what they say, what they do (or don't do) in response to issues raised by employees, what signals they give, and what messages they impart. Work on improving leadership EQs. Work on boosting employee morale. Work at listening better, harder, longer. 'See' your employees and believe that they want to do the best job possible. Root out dishonesty, negativity, and sarcasm in management, and do not try to preserve the status quo at all costs. Change is not a bad word. Believe that you can change, work at changing things, and change will happen. Not overnight, but slowly, and that may be the best kind of change because it will reflect thoughtfulness, objectivity, and clarity about the problem of passive-aggressive leadership.

References cited

1. Diagnostic and Statistical Manual of Mental Disorders DSM-IV Publisher: American Psychiatric Association; Fourth edition January 15, 1994.

2. How to Stop Passive-Aggressive Behavior in the Workplace: Power Phrases for Dealing with Passive-Aggressive Coworkers and Employees.
   http://www.speakstrong.com/articles/workplace-communication/howtostoppassiveaggressivebehavior.html

3. A Short Guide to a Happy Life by Anna Quindlen. Publisher: Random House; 1 edition October 31, 2000.

Websites of Interest

- Advanced Leadership Consulting
  http://www.leadershipconsulting.com/the-insidious-executive.htm
- Business First
  http://louisville.bizjournals.com/memphis/stories/2008/03/31/smallb4.html
- The Columbia Consultancy
  http://www.columbiaconsult.com/pubs/v28_jun02.html
- Construction Business Owner Magazine
  http://www.constructionbusinessowner.com/topics/people-management/understand-and-manage-passive-aggressive-employees.html
- Emoclear http://www.emoclear.com/personalityclusters.htm
- Executive Coaching & Consulting Associates http://www.exe-coach.com
- Managed Healthcare Executive
  http://managedhealthcareexecutive.modernmedicine.com
- Ptypes Personality Types http://www.ptypes.com
- Creative Conflict Resolutions
  http://www.norafemenia.com/bio.html

Made in the USA
Lexington, KY
17 May 2014